Why Can't I Be *Happy?*

From
Self-Hate
to
Self-Love

Dr. Jamila Khan

Why Can't I Be Happy? From Self-Hate to Self-Love

© Copyright 2020 Dr. Jamila Khan
Revised edition

For more information, email Whycantibehappy@gmail.com
ISBN:
978-1-7358807-3-0 Ebook Kindle
978-1-7358807-5-4 Paperback
978-1-7358807-6-1 Hardback

Dedication

I wish to thank all those who have given me lemons. Without you, I would not have had a reason to learn how to make lemonade.

Special thanks to Father Shaffick Mohammed for planting the seed of compassion.

To all my family members living and deceased, I love you all. Thank you for providing me with precious memories and keeping our family exciting and fun.

To my children, Sasha Laila and Omar Aziz, you two are my everything, and everything I do, I do it for you. I am so proud of each of you for living a life that honors yourself and God and always reaches for the stars without fear. I love you, I see you, and I appreciate you both beyond words.

To all my coaches and teachers, if I'm a visionary, it's because I'm standing on the shoulders of giants.

And to all the women across the globe who are suffering in the darkness, know you are good enough, and you have the right to be happy and the right to live your life as you wish.

Contents

Dedication iii

Introduction vii

Chapter One 1

    Buried Anger 1

Chapter Two 10

    The Early Years...10

    An English Rose 11

    The Goat Herder 12

Chapter Three...18

    The Yellow Brick House on the Hill 18

    Naani's House... 22

Chapter Four..26

    City of Lights.. 26

    Fears Become Reality...31

    Puppy Love 33

Chapter Five...35

    Breaking the Rules...35

    Taking Chances 39

Chapter Six 47

    A Wholesome Life 47

A Prince and A Princess 50

A Blessed Life...53

Chapter Seven 56

What's Wrong with Me? 56

Chapter Eight..63

Finding My Power 63

Is This the Truth or My Interpretation? 70

Chapter Nine 75

Clarity, Change, and Transformation..75

Defining Love, Compassion, and Trust 82

Chapter Ten 87

A Whole New World 87

Judaism 91

Christianity 92

Islam 97

Chapter Eleven.. 101

The Spiritual Journey of the Soul.. 101

The Traveling Soul 107

Chapter Twelve 110

Love at Last 110

Epilogue.. 115

Contributors and Resources. 119

Introduction

"The relationship you have with yourself sets the tone for every other relationship you have." —*Robert Holden*

When we think of PTSD (Post-traumatic stress disorder), we associate the word with veterans, refugees from war-torn countries, or those who experienced a significant life crisis. Sometimes, those who have PTSD have experienced a trauma such as rape or a horrible accident that claimed a loved one's life.

But, there is another form of trauma that takes place in the subtleties of life. That's the kind of trauma that leaves you feeling ashamed, embarrassed, or stigmatized. Such trauma could stem from your religion, birthplace, the way you speak, an accent, or skin tone. And sometimes, it could stem from your socioeconomic status, your culture, or your own family. People who are most vulnerable to subtle trauma include, but are not limited to, people with varied gender identities, LGBTQIA+ communities, immigrants, and minorities.

Unlike recognizable trauma, which only needs to occur once to develop symptoms of PTSD. Subtle trauma is not a one-time occurrence. Instead, it's a built-up of traumatic events that add up and eventually explode. Repeatedly being called names like *stupid* or *good-for-nothing* leaves an emotional scar on the psyche. Being slapped around or severely beaten and punished, even though it may be accepted in some cultures, can also create doubts about love and trust in one's mind. Moving too many times creates instability in a young child's life too. Or being denied fundamental rights like education, or the right to make your own decision, can leave you feeling unloved and insecure, which boomerangs into self-hate. It would be unfair to say that subtle trauma is more or less traumatic than recognizable trauma because the psychological results are the same.

The National Mental Health Association (NMHA), in conjunction with The American Psychological Association (APA), has called everyday trauma in our communities: A critical mental health issue---A public health crisis. Due in part to the inability to recognize the subtleties of abuse. Victims of subtle trauma tend to over-look the abuse normalizing the behavior. They tend to stuff and hide their feelings of unworthiness, humiliation, or feeling unloved until they eventually explode. Often, when we hear about horrible incidents such as a school shooting or other violent acts, the perpetrator is described as "He/she was so quiet" or "He/she was a nice person, always keeping to themselves." Seemingly ordinary people may be experiencing the effects of PTSD without knowing that trauma had occurred. This unknown and undiagnosed mental health condition is over-looked and labeled as "a difficult person."

I'm of Trinidadian heritage and no stranger to the poor language choices and attitudes that permeate the culture. A common Trinidadian (Trini) habit is to call others by their least desirable quality, like the boy who walks with a limp is called *Broke's* like he's broken. Or an overweight girl is called *Slim* or sometimes straight-up *Fatso*. As harmless as that may seem to some, it can cut deep. It can cause you to feel ashamed and embarrassed. Degrading someone for the way they look or punishing your children to the point of abuse in the name of discipline is subtle abuse leaving the victim to feel unworthy.

Having a traumatic background makes it challenging to fully enjoy life and be happy, even if your life has improved as an adult, and you've become successful. Untreated childhood trauma becomes deeply rooted, making you feel like there's a hole in your heart. Leaving you to ask the questions: "What's wrong with me? or Why can't I be happy?"

After becoming a parent, I worried whether I had learned the abuse pattern and would treat my children in the same way. This pattern of generational abuse often gets overlooked as a form of abuse, making it widely accepted.

I was raised in a family and cultural environment that fostered shame and guilt. I was shamed not only for the things I did as a child but also for the way I was born. Family members bullied and humiliated me, making fun of my lazy eye, which led to my nickname, *Cokey Eye*.

I suffered years of physical and emotional abuse from my overstressed father in my early childhood; he has since passed away. I was deprived of an education and pressured by my cultural norms to get married at age eighteen. I was constantly teased, and others in my family often reminded me that my father did not like me. As a young girl, I spent time in and out of hospitals from beatings and other severe physical abuse. Those abusive incidents took a toll on my psyche, which led to self-destructive behaviors in early adulthood.

While some people operate out of fear, I operated out of shame, and it hurt. I was ashamed of myself, not because of something I did, but because other people told me I should feel ashamed. Those feelings made me hate myself, robbing me of my self-esteem and confidence. And as we know, hurt people tend to hurt other people.

At a young age, I had what looked like the perfect marriage to a wonderful husband, two beautiful and loving children, and in-laws who became closer to me than my own family. We lived a respectable life in an executive home, complete with a white picket fence, two cars, and financial stability. Yet, I found myself unable to feel completely happy. There was always that hole inside me, a pit filled with doubt, shame, mistrust, and fear. But no one understood me—not even me. I kept asking myself, *Why can't I be happy? What's wrong with me?*

Eventually, I was introduced to transformational learning, and that truly did transform my life. Tired of living with the constant sadness and the persistent dislike for myself and others, I decided to change. That meant taking responsibility and being accountable for my life. I've learned to reframe my trauma by examining the actual thing that happened, which helped me gain new insights and perspectives. I had to let go of the old meanings I had attached to events and people. This new outlook helped me to create meaningful moments and relationships of compassion, love, and inspiration to move forward.

Reframing my life as I have has freed me to create a life that I love. I continue teaching others to do the same. We all deserve to have a say in how our lives turn out. I know for sure that God did not create us to suffer or to be miserable. He created us from love to love and be loved. And it starts with self-love.

Living a transformed life has freed me from the blame game and enabled me to be accountable for my own happiness. I was set free when I realized that I've always had the power and choice to change my life. I returned to school to become a Pastoral Psychologist. Over the years, I've treated hundreds of girls and women from all different walks of life. At one point or another, they have all asked the questions, "Doc, what's wrong with me? Why can't I be happy?"

The truth is that there's nothing wrong with them, just as there was nothing wrong with me. What happened to us (me and them) was bad enough, but the meaning we gave to those events created negative stories about ourselves. And those stories were based on what other people did to us, intentionally or not. It's those stories that have kept us from true self-love.

Do you find yourself repeating the same mistakes? Perhaps no matter what you do, people still break your trust, or you keep getting your heart broken. When this continues to happen, we tend to say, "I'm so stupid" or "I should have known better" or "why me?" Yet, the truth is that this cycle continues not as a punishment but as a fundamental lesson that you must learn so that you can move on to the next stage of your spiritual journey. Similar to school, you must pass one grade to move onto the next. You must get a bachelor's degree before your master's and your master's before your doctorate. With each degree, the test is more difficult, but you're also more prepared. The key is to remember it's all happening *for you*, not *to you*.

Since becoming a psychologist, I've traveled to more than forty countries and spoken to women from different economic and religious backgrounds. Despite their various circumstances, many of these women expressed the same feelings of powerlessness, unloved, not being good enough, and self-hatred. All these feelings have hindered their happiness. Many of these women had attempted suicide or have had suicidal thoughts. This often led them to ask: "What's wrong with me? Or Why can't I be happy?"

If that sounds familiar to you, then you've come to the right place. I'll share my story—the good, the bad, and the ugly of recognizable and subtle trauma and how it affected my adult life. You are not alone; you are not crazy; there is nothing wrong with you. You, too, can overcome your trauma and be HAPPY: As long as you are willing to be true to yourself and honor your word. Recognizing that you currently have PTSD is the first step to realizing that there is nothing wrong with you. However, there are many things wrong with your abuser. Whether they perpetuate extreme or subtle trauma, they are hurt people living in pain. Unfortunately, they repeat what they know, and that is to hurt others. Sometimes it feels so familiar and comfortable to the abuser that they become oblivious to their afflicting pain.

This book is written to bring awareness to everyday trauma and its devastating effects. When such effects are left untreated, depression, anxiety, and a host of other mental and physical illnesses can occur.

I bring awareness to trauma and its effect through my personal stories of growing up in an abusive home and abusive culture. I was a victim of both subtle and outwardly recognizable trauma. Since then, I've learned to reframe my trauma by becoming clear on the facts of what exactly happened, create a new interpretation, and then filed it in the past. That empowered me to live in the present without the baggage of the past. I am focusing on what's in front of me. Like an artist with a blank canvas, I now design my future, free to create whatever future I want. I've overcome many obstacles to fulfill my dream of earning a doctorate. Now I'm traveling the world to empower women worldwide to live a life they love.

This book also offers tools and resources to help you overcome your trauma. Landmark Education, available through the Curriculum for Living, introduced me to the concept of transformation. I've learned to challenge my beliefs and old passed down ideologies and reexamine how I look at life. I've reframed my messy life into one that makes sense to me. My education, travels, and life experiences help carve out new meanings and new ways of looking at the world and its people. If you implement these tools in your life and create a life that makes sense to you, I guarantee that you will wake up every day and say, "I love the life I live." I have since 1994! I've woken up every day, and despite whatever situation I'm in, I'm able to say with sincerity that *I love the life I live.*

Ten years after the worst day of my life, the day I felt it was either divorce or suicide, I can honestly say that I love the life that I live. I've found God in the process. I've gained wisdom and knowledge over the years, learning to trust myself that everything happens for a reason, and it happens with God's timing, not ours. My purpose on earth is to learn lessons through a series of tests. If I don't pass a test, I have to repeat it until I learn the lesson because that lesson is essential to move on to the next phase in my spiritual journey.

I firmly believe that life on earth is a test, full of lessons. However, life's lessons are not linear. They are sporadic. You don't go through trauma, come out of it, get the lessons, and then move on. Some get the lessons immediately, but for others, it may come years afterward. It comes in the ah-ha moments.

Paying attention to those lessons and ah-ha moments will help you choose happiness and live a life you love. Awareness is key! Are you being angry, sad, and upset, or are you being compassionate, happy, and loving? Self-awareness is crucial to your journey to a happier life.

That's what I want for everyone, for every human being—to live the life that they love. A life that is free from mental anguish, physical abuse, and spiritual deprivation. I hope that everyone who reads this book will walk away feeling moved and inspired to live the life they want with grace. So, reach for the stars, as long as you're trying, you are succeeding. Failure only comes when you don't bother to try. A life full of big dreams is the life we were all born to have.

I'm sharing my personal story hoping that every reader will discover how to recognize their trauma, embrace it, and take the valuable lessons it was meant to teach you. For in doing so, you learn to become loving, compassionate, and forgiving. You will grow by challenging your belief system, and your reflections will help you gain awareness of who you are. These are some of the gifts that trauma can provide if you are willing to put forth the effort.

Chapter One

"Unexpressed emotions will never die. They are buried alive and will come forth later in uglier ways." —*Sigmund Freud*

Buried Anger

Growing up, my older sister and I were beaten and called many names by my father. Somehow, I seem to have gotten the worst of it.

But nothing had prepared me for what was about to happen on a scorching summer evening in July 1973. It was a traumatic yet magical moment that set me on a new path—a path that killed my childhood but birthed my passion and purpose.

I was used to slaps flying across my face as I jumped in front of my mother, shielding her from my father's fury. But that July evening was different. My father was a fearful and neurotic boy, uncertain how to be a man, a husband, or a father. Suppressed from his buried anger, hurt, and disappointment, he panicked. He unleashed his frustrations while in a rage and did the unthinkable.

Ironically, that moment transported me to a path of unexpected compassion and forgiveness.

I was ten years old in 1973. My parents, my two sisters, and I lived in a low-income, diverse Latino neighborhood in Providence, Rhode Island. Our home was nestled on Broad Street, a short five blocks from Saint Joseph's Hospital, and across the street from the Providence fire station.

Our Broad Street apartment was within walking distance to everything—a school, a library, and a jewelry factory. Many restaurants, including a KFC at the far end of the street, their lit-up spinning barrel visible from our living room. Staring at the spinning barrel during the week, I prayed that Papa would bring home a bucket of fried chicken, which he sometimes did when money wasn't so scarce. It was one of my favorite treats, right behind a particular Chinese restaurant, Papa would occasionally treat the family.

Our apartment building occupied the corner of the block with perfect views up and down Broad Street. We lived between our Spanish neighbors below and the small attic apartment where an eighty-year-old man lived. We called him Uncle. Uncle became our means of transportation as neither of my Trinidadian parents knew how to drive.

Summer months brought on smells of hot, dry, and stagnant air that left everyone lazy and tired. There were wafts of island spices from impromptu barbeques serving up delectable food from make-shift grills. It was the smell of summer in the 1970s.

Our neighborhood bustled with Spanish conversations and broken English. Children rode their bikes while the older women sat lazily on their porches doing nothing, music blasting in the background. The men worked on their old jalopies as they harmlessly hassled the young girls. My family spoke a broken dialect of English, known as British-Trini. But that was normal in our neighborhood. Everyone either spoke broken English or no English at all. And for me, everyone sounded like they had an accent. Even the Americans sounded either Southern or strange.

It was an unlikely block to find a French seafood restaurant, but Martinique's was just across the street from our apartment. It wasn't a place that people from our neighborhood patron. The entrance was in the back of the restaurant off the side street. It was very exclusive, which for us meant only for the wealthy.

Despite our different circumstances, my family blended well with our neighbors. Our neighbors were mostly minorities with various shades of brown skin, and some were illegal. Many had lots of children or large extended families. During the summer months, while their parents worked, the children in our neighborhood were left alone at home or with a grandmother or neighbors.

Everyone knew each other, and people looked out for one another. "Papi, gimme a hand to move the table," a neighbor would say to a passerby. "Aye, no problem, amigo!" And people were helped. When someone in the neighborhood wanted to move, everyone helped—some with their cars making several trips, which took the entire day. Renting a moving truck was an unheard-of luxury that no one from our Broad Street neighborhood could afford.

My sisters and I wore hand-me-downs, with most of our clothes and furniture coming from the Salvation Army or giveaways from friends.

But that ended one day when our next-door neighbor, a ninety-two-year-old woman who lived across the hall from us, was found dead. Mama checked on her every day, but one day there was no answer. Mama didn't think much of it until the next afternoon when she knocked on the door, but there was still no answer. Worried, she and uncle decided to call the police.

The woman had one son who lived out of town, and he wanted to dispose of her things; he was eager for us to take anything we wanted. So, we took it all. We acquired antique couches with matching Chippendale chairs, seventeenth-century armoires, canopy beds with matching dressers, a sitting bench, and a beautiful mahogany dining room table.

These were great finds for having come to America with very little. My parents, sisters, and I originally moved to America in 1972. My father, Andy, had come to America two years earlier, then my mother, Sharon, joined him a year later. They'd left us (three children) in the care of my maternal grandmother, Naani, and my brother stayed with my paternal uncles and grandmother, Daadi. We are Muslims by birth, even though my parents did not practice any religion, except for not eating pork or drinking alcohol. Those restrictions kept us from accepting food from anyone.

However, that ended one day when my sister, Salma, and I shared our neighbor Ester's pepperoni pizza. Ester swore it was not pork. Not realizing that it was, we devoured it. "Pepperoni pizza is delicious," I said in agreement with my sister. So, the next time Papa took us shopping, he stopped to get us a slice of pizza. It was a typical Saturday treat after we finished our chores. I ordered my slice of pepperoni pizza, hardly containing my joy at my newfound delight.

"I'll have a slice of the pepperoni pizza, pl—"

Before I could finish ordering, a slap flew across my face so swiftly it left me dazed and confused.

"What the hell did you order?" Papa screeched as he now had one hand placed on my arm and his other hand ready to strike.

"Pepper-noni," I whimpered.

"Who the hell said you could eat that? That's pork. You want to eat pig?" he scolded me.

I cried, but mostly because I was even more disgusted by the fact that I'd eaten pork when devouring the pizza Ester had shared.

"Stop it!" I cried. "I won't eat it again."

"Then where did you eat that? Where did you eat pepperoni?" Papa's voice began to calm down.

This incident is embedded in my mind. To this day, I still always ask if there are pork products in any food that I order. Today, it's a lot easier to say I'm kosher than halal as almost everyone in America knows this Yiddish word's guidelines.

In our minority community, everyone worked, even the few black and white folks. Most of the women in my neighborhood had jobs as maids. But Mama worked at the old folks' home on the next block. She started in the kitchen in food prep and then became a dietitian. There were no degree or diploma requirements for the position. Mama didn't even know how to read. But she had an interest in nutrition and, in those days, her skills were good enough to land her the job.

Mama had always been health-conscious, preferring baked chicken to curry chicken. "It's healthier for you, Andy. All that oil isn't good for your heart," she'd say to Papa. Papa was a very hearty eater, but healthy eating was not his priority. It got to the point where he could no longer eat Mama's bland food; he asked Salma to take over the cooking duties in addition to our weekend chores.

The whole neighborhood seemed to be out enjoying the summer Saturday mornings. But for my sister and me, Saturday was cleaning day and changing the sheets, disinfecting everything with water and Clorox, and mopping with Pine-Sol.

Weary from all the chores, one day, I grumbled while picking up my mop, "Why do I have to mop the hallways? We're not the only one who uses them."

"Because we live here, and we are not nasty people," Mama replied in her pompous tone. "When you're done, don't forget to change the mattress liners." She continued.

Although my parents had to budget themselves and money was scarce, there was never a shortage of goodies in our home. It was always filled with lots of food, such as fresh-baked bread and pastries and cakes from the bakery. Armando, the Italian baker who owned the bakery on the first floor of our building, always brought up free treats at the end of the day. Papa also brought home many cuts of meats from his Italian friends in Federal Hill. They were terrific cuts of beef, lamb, goat, and chicken, all fresh from nearby farms. There were also more exotic parts like tripe, oxtails, or cow's feet. The Italian boys up in Federal Hill took good care of Papa, though it was an exclusive men's club.

A year after our family migrated to America, our visa expired. We were overstaying our visa and living illegally in the country. Papa was becoming increasingly paranoid that immigration officers would round him up without notice. That fear drove his furtive behavior, his anger, and his violent outbursts.

Staying one step ahead of his imaginary predators, we moved nine times within three years but all within the same community. Sometimes only houses away. We once moved from the third floor of one side of the building to the second floor of the other side of the same building. But our stay in the Broad Street apartment was the longest we lived in one place in Providence. That lasted an entire year.

Our neighborhood had a Spanish club, which became the hangout spot for adults. It was just a few blocks up the street. Ester was Salma's best friend. When Salma and Ester got together, they were always quiet and concentrated on their cooking skills because they had no interest in school. One day Ester's elder cousin Carlos dropped by to pick up a group of ladies headed for the club. Carlos was a twenty-three-year-old Antonio Banderas look-alike. He played the guitar and serenaded the middle-aged, underdressed mothers in the community. Those Spanish women were hard-working wives and mothers during the week, but they turned into feisty, fun, and sexy women on the weekends.

Despite their age difference, Salma and Carlos became smitten with each other, giving Carlos a reason to visit more frequently. Night after night, he would stand outside singing and playing the guitar to lure Salma to the kitchen window. Salma and I would dig through our assigned trash bags where we kept our clothes—ready to move at a moment's notice—so we could find her the prettiest dress to wear. Salma was very shy and quiet, so her only attention-grabbing factor was to look pretty while he sang to her.

It was on one of these serenading occasions on a sweltering evening in July 1973 that my world changed forever.

Our home had no air conditioning and little breeze, which made the evening almost unbearable. My sister and I were not allowed to talk to boys as Papa strictly forbade a boyfriend-girlfriend relationship, calling it the worst part of American culture. She had to see Carlos in secrecy.

On that hot evening, Mama was taking a bath to cool off in our bathroom, which was just off the kitchen. Liz, the baby of the family, was four and napping within Salma's view in the bedroom off the kitchen toward the back of the apartment. The bedroom had a window facing the fire station.

That evening, Papa entered our home through the back door. I was tucked away in the kitchen pantry, hidden from view behind the beaded curtains, and curled up with my book. I watched as he went into the kitchen carrying a package of oxtail wrapped in crisp white paper and tied with twine. His heavy feet thumped the floor, which made me anxious. I listened as he tossed it into the refrigerator. He then dragged his weary bones to change out of his work clothes before entering the front room. He turned on the TV and dropped into his green rocking chair. Once he settled in, he'd reach down the side of the chair to feel for the handle of his cutlass (a short sword) peeking out from underneath.

The cutlass was always with him at home—under the chair when he watched TV, in the bathroom with him when he showered, under the bed while he slept. There was no mention of it. Perhaps it was a symptom of his paranoia. For Trinis, the cutlass was the weapon of choice. It was used in the cane fields and on many farm jobs. They were plentiful, either store-bought or homemade. And it was not uncommon in a Trini household as it's used for home and personal protection. You might say the cutlass is to Trini what a .38 caliber is to Americans.

That evening, like all others, Salma fixed Papa's dinner. She has pulled away from her boyfriend for a minute, and, anxious to get back to him, she forgot Papa's drink as she carried his plate into the living room. Papa's eyes were fixated on the television report about the Watergate scandal. His attention elsewhere, he didn't even notice she came into the room.

Minutes later, Papa shouted in an irritated voice, "Gimme something to drink."

"Sorry," Salma shouted back. "Coming."

She quickly grabbed a heavy ceramic mug out of the cabinet. The kind they gave away for free in the '70s at gas stations when you filled up your tank. She hurriedly poured Coke into the mug, forgetting to add the ice and setting it on the counter. She's determined not to get pulled away from Carlos again.

"Eyes," Salma cried out. That was one of my nicknames, a mockery for my lazy eye.

"Eyes!" Salma called again. I was unable to ignore her any longer as I hid in the corner, reading my book. A wasteful activity, according to my father. He preferred that I spend my time doing something useful, like cooking or cleaning.

Sighing while folding the page to create a marker, I jumped up from the floor to come around the corner and grab the big mug off the counter. Even as I sailed into the living room, I was distracted by my book. I was reading about the women of Rajasthan, India, and falling madly in love with the splendor of their colorful culture. I yearned for the day I could visit India and see those colorful landscapes. Lost in my thoughts, I placed the drink without ice on the table in front of Papa, then hurriedly tried to return to my book. But I did not make it back to the kitchen.

Walking a couple of steps away from Papa, a loud sound like the crack of a whip burst in the air as the sensation of a swift breeze grazed my ankle. Stumbling down the corridor, I fell about five steps later. Lying there in confusion, I stared at the ceiling. Seconds later, blood began pitching up to the ceiling, droplets falling back on my thighs. As I followed the trail of blood, I saw my left ankle dangling from my foot in a pool of blood. Despite not processing what had happened, I didn't panic. I didn't even cry. Instead, I felt lifted, carried aloft. Never had I experienced such a feeling—a sense of total calmness and peace.

I saw everyone rushing toward me, and then I realized something had happened. From the corner of my eyes, I saw my mother frantically running out of the bathroom, half-covered, screaming, "What happened? What happened?!"

Papa leaped from his chair and ran towards Mama, screaming her nickname, "Doll! Doll!" as he realized that he injured me. In his anger that always seemed to be right there, like a ticking time bomb, he'd lost his temper to the slightest trigger. His hot drink in the already warm apartment triggered him to throw the mug behind me as I walked away. The mug hit the wood molding surrounding the doorway, broke, and hit my ankle, cutting it deeply.

Panic and tears filled my mother's eyes as she surveyed the scene. Gripped with fear, and dripping wet as she looked at me, she wept, "What did you do, Andy? Look what you did!"

Salma covered her mouth as she buried her head in her palms in disbelief. Then she steered Liz back to her bedroom and away from the carnage. Salma called out to the firemen across the street. "My sister's bleeding!" she shouted with panic in her voice. "Please come and help!" she pleaded.

Mama, still in shock, leaned over me and whispered an all too familiar phrase, "Don't put your father in trouble. Say the Coke bottle fell on your foot."

I understood exactly what she meant. She wanted to protect her husband. Because if immigration caught him, we would all be deported. And that was not an option.

All the neighbors were outside watching as they carried me off to the hospital, but no one batted an eye. This incident did not raise any child abuse issues—not within our community or at the hospital.

The doctor and nurse rushed me into the emergency room. I overheard them talking to my father. "She'll be admitted for a couple of days, but right now, we have to get her stitched up," one doctor said as they rushed me off to the operating room. It was the first time I saw my father cry. Perhaps he was scared that I would spill the beans. Or perhaps my hospitalization made him realize the gravity of the situation.

In the operating room, there were conversations between the staff, but it meant nothing to me. The emotional bliss that I fell into felt safe. My calmness seemed to concern the doctors. "She's very quiet," one doctor said to the nurse. "See if you can get a response from her" as he worked on my ankle.

The nurse came over and looked down at my face. "Are you okay, honey?"

Smiling, I looked up at her. "Yeah, I'm okay. Just talking to the angels."

"She's conscious, but she's delirious," reported the nurse.

Delirious? I smiled.

The truth was that I had never been more lucid in my life. My spirit was light and unencumbered. A perfect sense of clarity and peace—without any pain or worry—washed over me. And I knew that if I let go, I would fall into the loving arms of the angels who were right there to catch me.

A bright beam of light shone down on me from above. The light was so soft, almost tactile. Its primary purpose was to keep me warm as if it were a fluffy blanket, safe and comfortable. It was keeping me safer and more secure than I'd ever felt in my life. I was surrounded not only by the angels but also by God himself.

The doctors were dressed in scrubs with surgical masks, and they were holding large needles. The smell of medicine filled the air, and the fear of not knowing how much blood I'd lost didn't faze me. I didn't see my circumstance from a distance as people have described in an out-of-body experience. Instead, I did not leave my body; I was wrapped in warmth, love, and comfort, totally at peace.

Anger never entered my mind or heart, only sadness. I never wondered why my father did it. Instinctively, I knew why. I knew that's how he got when he was mad. I knew that he couldn't control his temper. In my heart, I knew that my father loved me. But that night, it didn't matter. What mattered was my profound sense of compassion for my father. I wondered what made him so angry, so full of hatred. And I wondered what happened to the father who'd sung under the plum tree every night for the villagers back home in Trinidad. I missed that, Papa. I missed falling asleep to his melodious voice.

Chapter Two

"In the happiest of childhood memories, our parents were happy too."—*Robert Breault*

The Early Years

Trinidad and Tobago, known as the Sister Islands, is the last and smallest island of the West Indies in the Caribbean Sea. It's situated about seven miles off the coast of Venezuela. It has been settled by the Spaniards, the French, the Dutch, and the British. A sprinkle of different ethnic groups such as Chinese, Syrians, and Lebanese also dropped in to bask in its beauty.

Most of Trinidad and Tobago's earlier immigrants came from Grenada, Martinique, and Dominica. These early settlers formed their communities in Laventille and Champs Fleur's communities, bringing their French food and culture and a more peaceful religious community. In 1844, the British government allowed the Indian workers from various parts of India to immigrate as indentured servants. They worked for menial pay and were given a land plot in exchange for their return passage to India.

The Indian settlers chose the countryside so they could work the land. Inadvertently this separated the villages into the Afro-Trinis and the Indian-Trinis.

An English Rose

Sharon, my mother, grew up in Claxton Bay on the south side of the country. She lived in a beautiful yellow concrete British-style home with five bedrooms, a living room, and a dining room. There were a kitchen and a complete bathroom upstairs. Downstairs there was another kitchen that opened to a hammock area, which included a bedroom with a bathroom and pool area. The house sat on acres of land with cows, goats, sheep, and horses. There was even a separate area for the chickens and ducks, which included their own wading pool. The yard was laden with every fruit tree imaginable—mangoes of every variety, chenet, zaboca, plums, pomerac, sapodilla, bananas, figs (green bananas), oranges, limes, and lemons. There were lush, fresh herb gardens with pepper trees, pudina plants, thyme, shadow-beni, and chives next to the vegetable gardens that grew an array of roots and fresh vegetables.

There was even a housemaid we called Didi, the Hindi word for big sister. Didi did everything, including taking care of my mother and later us kids.

Mama's daily routine as a young unmarried woman was to sit in her upstairs gallery. Under the coolness of fans, she created beautiful needlepoint works of art. Her favorite flower was the English rose, which she artfully crafted on pillowcases, scarves, and her signature white cotton dress. Her simple passion done completed effortlessly.

Mama's green thumb was evident in her beautiful English garden in the front yard, which draped down the side yard, lining the winding, pitched walkway that led to the house's open courtyard. Her garden bloomed with English roses and fragrant English lavender, ferns, and baby's breath. The freshness of English lavender mixed with scents of curry greeted you as you entered the yard.

Mama was contented living in her world with every decision being made for her. She was surrounded by people who loved and adored her. She never attended school because she didn't want to. And no one made her. Thus, she never learned to read or write.

Several suitors came from Europe over the years to ask for Mama's hand in marriage, but not wanting to leave her house and family, she refused all proposals.

One day Aunty Kay, the woman Mama knew as her mother and who raised her, made yet another choice for Mama. Without asking, Aunty Kay arranged my mother's marriage.

Papa worked in his family's butchery business, and he and his brothers shopped for livestock during the week. One day Papa ended up at Aunty Kay's farm. Papa used to fondly tell the story.

> We were driving down Soledad Road, and as we took the bend, I could not miss this majestic house sitting on a hill. I thought, *Yes! They will have some good animals.* We drove up to the house, and I saw Sharon sitting on her rocking chair in the upstairs gallery working on her needlepoint. I instantly fell in love with her. She looked like a porcelain doll. Doll became her nickname, and I quickly made a purchase for some animals and then boldly asked Aunty Kay if her daughter was available for marriage. Kay agreed and immediately prepared the engagement without asking her daughter.

My parents were married in a grand Islamic celebration at Aunty Kay's house. Mama's cousins used to recall the lavishness of the wedding: "We washed our hands in cream soda."

Following Indian culture and traditions, my mother, as a new bride, moved to her husband's parents' house in Pasea Village, Tunapuna, in the northern part of Trinidad. He lived with his mom (my Daadi or paternal grandmother), father (my Daada or paternal grandfather), and a handful of his siblings.

"The first time I saw my new home, the house of my in-laws, I cried. I could not believe that was my new life," my mother sadly recalled.

The Goat Herder

Papa belonged to an Indian village consisting of mostly Hindus and Muslims. The oldest of twelve children, he was a respected elder. No one spoke back to him or questioned his authority, and he was always consulted on family decisions. He was known as Bhai, the Hindi word for brother. No one younger than him smoked or drank alcohol in his presence or called him by his name as a sign of respect. He wasn't a drinker, but he was known for holding a cigarette while singing or whistling a tune. He was well-liked and friendly with everyone, known for his fair dealings and earning people's trust.

At that time, meat was served only on special occasions, holidays, and Sundays if one could afford it. The Tunapuna market was one of the busiest markets in the North and provided a handsome profit for the family. Papa did the negotiating from buying the animals to selling the meat in the market, but he didn't participate in the slaughtering.

"Your father never killed the animal because he's afraid to take a life," Mama adamantly stated. "Your father cried and couldn't sleep for days the first time he saw his brothers cut the throat of a goat. It disturbed him to see the goat suffering, and he thought it was inhumane."

As the baby of the family, the moment I saw Papa walking down the dirt road singing and whistling old Indian tunes, I would rush to embrace him. He'd scoop me up and carry me to safety in his muscular arms. Papa was very handsome with a strong jawline, deep inset eyes, and straight pearly white teeth with one gold canine tooth. He stood about five feet, seven inches, and weighed around one hundred and eighty pounds. But little me was afraid of his tattoos. His right arm bore a tattoo of the ace of hearts, homage to his love of cards. (He was particularly fond of a card game called All Fours, which is indigenous to Trinidad.) A Playboy bunny tattoo adorned his left arm. Despite his intimidating tattoos, his best feature was his smile, followed by his melodious voice.

When all the neighborhood children gathered in our yard in the evenings to play, Papa would often treat them to ice cream from the ice cream truck. Well, in Trinidad, it was an ice cream bicycle. It was a real treat for them and us. Sometimes Papa would call all the children to sit under the plum tree with the adults to tell us ghost stories. He was hilarious and had nicknames for all the children, semi-sarcastic ones, of course. The ultra-skinny and frail boy he'd called Sampson. "Show us those muscles, Sampson," he'd say. Sampson, grinning ear to ear, would flex his little muscles with pride, believing he was big and strong.

Papa was affectionately teased as he serenaded my mom with old Indian love songs. In the evenings when the children weren't around, Papa would gather under the plum tree in the front yard to sing. It didn't take long for the neighbors to join in, bringing tea and sweets as they listened to him sing the latest Indian songs and tell stories. My cousins, my sister, and I would play and whisper as we listened to his soothing voice until we fell asleep.

In the new setting of life with her in-laws, Mama began developing insecurities. She did not feel welcomed or well-liked. My mother is quiet and reserved, and that was her saving grace. She wasn't used to bickering or harsh speaking. Being a semi-princess, she'd always been treated gently.

Daadi's house was a flat one-story ranch-style dwelling made of mud with no indoor plumbing or electricity. It consisted of a large living room in the center, the walls decorated with pictures of Bollywood movie stars, which Daadi loved. A few chairs were pushed against the walls, leaving the room's center empty for the children to sit. Some years after my mother's arrival, electricity came to the area. Papa's brother pulled those lines into the home, which provided the light and luxuries like a television and a refrigerator. Surrounding the living room were bedrooms for the twelve children, and one reserved for Daadi and Daada. Several siblings shared a bedroom except for the married ones; they shared a bedroom with their wife and children.

Respecting the honor of Papa being the oldest, my grandparents built an extension onto the back of the house, which ran the house's length. It consisted of three blocks of rooms. One block was used as a bedroom with two queen-sized mattresses, jammed up against each of the walls, which created a small walkway in the middle. There were three windows, one on each wall. One window overlooked the ravine at the back of the house. Another window opened to the slaughter area and the animal's pen, while the third window was on the inside wall opening up to the main house. The second block was used as a sewing room for Mama, who sewed all our clothes. There was also a table, which was later used as a desk for homework. And a twin bed with a tall dresser at the end of the bed for Bobby (my brother). The third block was the kitchen. Mama was given the privilege of cooking only for her family except for Sunday's lunch: A extended family event.

Sunday mornings were my favorite, and they were incredibly fun at Daadi's house. The air seemed to burst with excitement. Adults paid little attention to the children; everyone else was busy doing their Sunday chores. My uncles were busy slaughtering the animals. Bobby was getting the cuts of meat ready for the market because everything from the animal was sold for a profit—the head, blood for sausages, bones for soup, tripe, even the skin which made great leather.

There was a public pipe stand with running water located on the banks of Daadi's yard. The pipe stand provided water for everyone on the street; people could bring their buckets and fill it up as much as they wanted. Sometimes you'd see mothers bringing their children to bathe under the pipe stand. My uncles ran piping from the stand into their property, making things easier for the butchery business. Everything was washed into the ravine, which laid stagnant until it rained, filling the ravine and pushing the water downstream.

Mama's job for the butcher operations was to clean the goat or sheep tripe; it was a chore she shared with her sisters-in-law. They sat around the pipe stand, cleaning the tripe, often complaining. Mama constantly repeated, "He brought me here to clean shit. This is what my life has become." She'd utter those words most of her life.

Even as a little girl, I was given chores in the business. My job was to carry the blood to the market across a busy highway, about a mile away from home. I made about two trips per day, rushing to the market before the blood clot. There was no time to delay. But I loved making those trips. It made me feel important, like I contributed. And all the way walking up the road, Indian music played on the radio. Sunday was the big day when Indian music played all day long.

When I got to the market, Papa was always there to greet me. He sold meat at the market. The customers trusted him because he'd tell them if the meat was soft or chewy. "This goat is a ram goat, so it's a little tough. I couldn't get a baby goat this week, but I'll save you some as soon as I get it."

Then he'd wink and smile. His charm helped him be the first to hang the SOLD-OUT sign. But don't be fooled into thinking he was innocent. Papa had lots of girlfriends.

One of Mama's favorite stories to tell was this one. Perhaps the shy, quiet girl finally felt empowered because she reacted. And for the first time, her in-laws stood up for her.

> I was about six years old, and my mother was nearly full-term with my little sister. We were walking back from the Sunday morning market close to noontime. Daadi and her daughters-in-law had finished making lunch. I could smell the delicious curry goat mixed with the aroma of dal (split peas) and fresh-cut tomatoes and cucumbers for the salad. And the crème de la créme: a whole bottle of Solo, the country's leading

soft drink. I had the entire bottle to myself; I didn't even have to share. Banana or white Solo were my favorites. These were the fragrances, ambiance, and treats we got on Sundays.

We were only one house away, and suddenly Mama let go of my hands and angrily grabbed a rock as she pushed me out of the way. A neighbor came out of nowhere, scooped me up, and carried me off. We safely watched the scene unfold from her yard. Mama saw my father's girlfriend walking into Daadi's yard. Furious at her audacity, my mother picked up a rock and aimed it at the girlfriend, striking the woman's ankle and breaking her foot. My aunts rushed to Mama's aid, getting her safely inside while Daadi pounced on the woman, vowing to kill her all the while spewing curses and insults. It was the last time my father was known to have had a girlfriend.

Daada never joined his sons in the butchery business. Instead, he sold roasted peanuts, roasted chickpeas known as channa, and roasted corn finely ground and mixed with sugar called jil-le-bebe at the two cinemas in town, the Monarch and Palladium. I didn't know Daada well, except that he worked a lot, many times taking my older brother Bobby with him. Bobby was the oldest grandson, and Daada's fondness often shielded Bobby from his uncles' unwarranted beatings. Luckily for the rest of the family, having Daada working at the cinema allowed the family access to the latest movies.

I was six years old when I saw my first American movie, *The Ten Commandments*. We arrived late because as we walked into the cinema, the scene playing on the big screen was the one where Miriam's pushing the basket into the river then hiding in the marshland to see where it would end up. Nodding off after that, the next time I looked up at the screen, I saw the most beautiful woman, and she took my breath away. Sephora, played by Yvonne De Carlo, was sitting in Mount Sinai's foothills talking to Moses. I was mesmerized and thought Sephora to be the most striking woman I'd seen. She became my idea of beauty—simple, exotic, soft brown skin, and soft-spoken with lots of *Noor*, the Arabic word for light.

Papa and his family did not practice any religion, although they were all born into the Islamic faith. As such, Papa had no religious or secular education. No one ever prayed or fasted during the holy month, but they celebrated Eid, the festival at the end of Ramadan. Lots of food, music, family, and friends made for a wonderful celebration. Eid became one of the many holidays celebrated in Daadi's house, along with Diwali, the Hindu festival of lights, and Christmas, among others. They celebrated all the religious holidays without the sacred part.

During the earthquake of 1969, it was the first time I realized that we were Muslims rather than Hindu. I'm not sure what the earthquake measured on the Richter scale. But the villagers were wailing during the night. My sisters and I huddled up in the bed. The beds were jammed up against the inside wall that opened into the main house and the backroom connecting Daadi's bedroom. We opened the window while the house was rattling and huddled together, scared to death, not understanding what was happening.

My parents were busy helping Bobby, who screamed, "The press is falling on me!" Daadi wailed "Ya Allah Pak! Ya Allah Pak" in Arabic, the language of the Quran, meaning "Oh my God."

Soon after that night, a picture of the Buraq hung on the wall. Buraq is a mythical creature from the heavens that transported the Prophet Muhammad from Mecca to Jerusalem and back during the night journey known as Isra and Mi'raj. Even as a little girl, this picture caught my attention. I wondered so many things. *Why is he half horse and half man? Who is he? What's his purpose?* No one could tell me anything about it because they didn't know themselves. To them, it was only a religious picture.

Of Daadi's twelve children, there were ten boys and two girls. The eldest daughter was married and had moved to her husband's home a couple of villages away. She had three children and was the first to move to America, buy a home, and become a U.S. citizen. In 1970, the remaining siblings, my brother Bobby, and my grandparents all had plans in the works to come to America.

A year after the earthquake, some of my uncles had made a break for the United States. Several had already left in search of a better life in America.

Papa, too, was trying his luck at the American Dream. Even though he didn't get a green card, he did get a one-year visa. It was renewed for another year, and Mama got a visa too. They left for America, leaving my sisters and me in the care of Aunty Kay.

Chapter Three

"My memories of feeling loved was when I also felt accepted."
—*Jamila Khan*

The Yellow Brick House on the Hill

Aunty Kay's house in the South was much quieter. The area was less populated and more easygoing with its rolling hills and lots of greenery. My first memory of Aunty Kay's was when I was about four years old, and my mother took me with her to visit her family in Claxton Bay.

It was a rainy day, and we got out of the taxi in front of this majestic yellow brick house on a sloping hill. It was a spectacle to see everyone with such excitement and joy running to the street, shouting, "Boobee's here! Boobee's here!" Boobee was their nickname for Mama for reasons unknown to this day. Aunties and cousins unknown and unfamiliar to me picked me up, kissing and hugging me as if I were one of their own. It felt like I came home; it's my first memory of feeling accepted and completely loved.

With both of my parents living in America, living with Aunty was like a vacation. My sisters and I lived in a beautiful home with all the best amenities and no chores—nothing to do but play and have fun with our cousins. We went to school with our cousins, came home, threw our books wherever, and played until dinner time. Didi prepared dinner, picked up our books, and ironed our uniforms, getting them ready for the next day. Life was so joyous that I barely missed my parents.

Aunty Kay never declared whether she was Hindu, as she tried in vain to practice Islam. On many occasions, my cousins, sisters, and I watched Aunty Kay preparing herself in a white sari and offering puja, the Hindu morning prayer ritual, under a particular mango tree. That tree bears a mango appropriately known as the ten-pound mango. But more remarkable was the colossal cobra snake that lived around the tree. As kids, we were warned never to go or play around the tree, and we never did.

Visible from the house's back stairs, the mango tree was easy to observe from a safe distance. Once, we saw the cobra drinking the milk which Aunty Kay laid out for him as an offering. We jokingly teased that the cobra was Aunty Kay's deceased husband reincarnated.

Aunty Kay also allowed us to decorate the house for Diwali, the Hindu festival of lights. The house's layout with its winding walkway and the wraparound gallery was the perfect canvas to create the most magical setting. We used diya's, or small clay cups filled with oil and a wick, to light up the estate. When all decked out with the diya's, Aunty Kay's house was a magical beacon of light visible from the bottom of the hill.

On other occasions, Aunty Kay tried to host the traditional Islamic Moulood, a tradition passed down from the Persians to Indian Muslims, with the Indian Muslims bringing it to Trinidad. Over time, culture crept in, and a new tradition was born. Many Muslims feel the Moulood function keeps them connected to the religion and the community. Guests gather to recite the Quran and thank Allah (God) for whatever purpose the Moulood was being held. Muslims will choose a Moulood function to celebrate birthdays, anniversaries, promotions, or someone recovering from an illness. The recitation is then followed by singing religious songs known as Qasida's, traditional Arabic poetry honoring the Quran's people. The Moulood ended with a dua (prayer) before everyone indulged in an elaborate meal prepared by the host.

Like many Muslims in Trinidad, Aunty Kay was not formally educated in Islam, meaning she had not studied Islam or have read the Quran to know exactly what Islam teaches. Instead, religious practices were inherited from their parents or caretakers. The mixtures of religions and cultures have crept in, creating new traditions mistakenly practiced as an Islamic ritual. One of these practices is Niyaz (pronounced-knee-arge), a smaller version of a Moulood function minus the singing and the length of the function. It involves only a few guests, Quran recitation, and dinner. What makes this ritual odd is that it's indigenous to Trinidad and contains many Hindu practices. As guests gather around to recite the Quran, a plate of food is placed in the middle and is considered "holy food." Then it's shared in tiny bits so everyone can get blessings from eating the holy food.

The idea of praying over something to receive a blessing is very un-Islamic as it assigns divine power to an object. Yet, even practicing Trini-Muslims swear by the niyaz function and are often offended when corrected.

My sister and I were enrolled at Sum Sum Hill elementary school alongside my cousins and many neighborhood children. I was in second standard (or second grade) and placed in Miss Jameela's class. Miss Jameela was tall with bronze skin and long black silky hair. She had full lips and a smile that reached her ears, showing off her perfect set of white teeth. Reserved and quiet, she spoke in a stern but soft tone. There was an air of mystery about her. Under her soft and innocent exterior, I could sense that she had a racy, edgy side. The teacher's uniform was a brown skirt (but Miss Jameela's was a mini) with a white shirt layered with a brown vest. She wore a scarf tied as a headband in her stylish way, typical of the '60s and reminiscent of the Indian movie star style. Miss Jameela fit my idea of a beautiful woman, and I aspired to be like her. A perfect balance of brains and beauty.

My school resembled a large one-room schoolhouse with no inside walls. The classrooms were set up facing the outer wall with a chalkboard leaving the middle as a walkway. Hanging from the ceiling over the class were our standards followed with the form or rank. Over my class hung 2A, second standard, and level A for those ranked in their studies' top ten.

My circle of friends at school included three boys and two girls. The two girls and I were the top three in class. Of the three boys, one was my cousin from Soledad Road. We rarely saw each other unless there was a family function, or sometimes during our Sunday visits.

At home, life was happy and enjoyable. Lazily, my cousins, Salma, and I walked home together after school, saying hello to everyone on the way.

"As-salaam Alaikum," we'd shout as we passed the homes. We knew everyone who lived in every house on the way to school. That's how it was in the islands. As we walked, villagers shouted out to us, "tell your grandmother I'll have two roosters for sale this Sunday if she wants them" or "come, come and take these tomatoes for your Naani."

Everyone knew what everyone else was cooking by the smell. There were whiffs of curry mangoes, and dal or curry peas with eddoes, a kind of sticky potato. Sometimes, the smell of roasting tomatoes or baigan (eggplant) filled the air. By the time I got home, I'd worked up an appetite and was starving. Luckily Didi never disappointed us.

As I approached Aunty Kay's house, I scattered my uniform from the front yard all the way upstairs. Then I'd toss down my books before changing into play clothes. Dashing down the back stairs to the outside kitchen, I'd smile as I rounded the corner to the glorious sight of Didi's delicatessen waiting for us—plates of aloo (potato) pies, preserved fruits, or bowls of fresh fruits like mangoes or caimet, and jamoon (sweets). Sometimes Grady, Aunty Kay's mom, would make yogurt from scratch. As the summer evenings lingered on, I was off to play cricket or pitch marbles with my cousins and the neighborhood kids. Sometimes we would climb up a mango tree, pick a half-riped mango, and make a chow by cutting up mangoes with salt, pepper, garlic, and culantro or shadow-beni.

Aside from the radio playing Indian songs all day, the smell of Sunday mornings was distinct. Curry aromas mixed with the scent of fresh herbs and chicken and the smokiness of the Chula (small clay stove). There was also the tangy smell of the freshly squeezed lime juice, made from the bountiful garden's delectable limes. Fresh cut flowers from Mama's garden were placed on the formal dining room table. Music and chattering from the neighbors created an ambiance like no other. Meat was eaten only on Sundays, and everyone was limited to two pieces per person. Those two pieces were the most delicious and treasured part of Sunday's lunch.

After lunch, all the girls in the neighborhood got dressed in their Sunday best. It was the only occasion we had to get dolled up as we embarked on our Sunday walk. Didi and the neighbors all took that leisurely walk down Sum Sum Hill to Soledad Road, visiting friends on the way. They were carrying goodies like fresh milk, eggs, or fresh vegetables and herbs from the garden. Sometimes they would bring Grady's specialties, homemade yogurt called

Dahi, and homemade coconut oil for the elders or poorer neighbors down Soledad Road.

Sunday walks were the highlight of my week. It was freeing to have some independence from the elders and soak in all the fashion of everyone's Sunday best. Even so, all good things must come to an end. And after the school year ended, so did our stay with Aunty Kay.

Naani's House

My mother returned from America at the end of her one-year visa and moved us up the road to her biological mother or Naani's house. My mother was born out of wedlock and given to Aunty Kay (Naani's sister), who had been recently widowed at that time. My mother's biological father is believed to have been from a wealthy Syrian family, giving my mother her distinct look of fair skin and greenish-gray eyes that we called cat eyes. My mother didn't know her true identity until she was well into her late thirties.

My Naani (maternal grandmother) was a practicing Muslim who spoke fluent English and Urdu and recited the Quran in Arabic. She married a man of mixed-race, of Indian and African descent. Naana (maternal grandfather) was very quiet, peaceful, and kind. I don't recall what he sounded like as he mostly smiled and nodded.

Naana was a truck driver and got up around four o'clock every morning. Although that sounds early, most people on the island started their day around that time. Naani woke up every morning to pray the first prayer of the day before sunrise, called Fajr before she fixed breakfast, and packed a lunch for Naana. Then off he went, returning around six or seven in the evening.

Like a well-oiled engine, Naana's routine ran smoothly. He'd park the truck on the side yard and walk straight to the outside shower, where clean clothes hung on the adjacent mango tree waiting for him. His dirty clothes dropped on the ground as he walked gracefully to the gallery, not uttering a word but always wearing a smile as he sat patiently waiting for Naani to bring him his dinner, which she had ready and waiting.

Naani's house was on the main road across from the largest rum shop in Claxton Bay. The gallery offered the perfect spot to people watch from a safe distance. We didn't have a television, so the radio was our only connection to the outside world. Naana listened to the BBC news to stay current with the news both in Trinidad and the world.

Naani's house had rules, with chores and no maid to pick up after us. My aunt, Mama's half-sister in her mid-twenties, did most of the housework while Naani tended to the animals and gardens. One of Naani's rules was that you were not allowed to enter the yard without saying "As-salaam Alaikum," the Islamic greeting meaning "peace be with you," and you did not dare enter until you heard the reply "Wa-Alaikum salaam," meaning "peace be with you too." I shouted it from the top of my lungs as I entered the yard because sometimes Naani was way out in the fields behind the house. My aunt and one of my uncles, and Naana were Christians, but they still followed her rules.

Everyone was in charge of preparing their own books and uniform for the next day. Didi wasn't there to pick up and organize our books from the yard. In the mornings, we had to make our beds and hang out our towels before having breakfast.

After returning home from school, I had to deliver food or picks from Naani's garden, which she shared with people in the village. For some people, those vegetables were all they had to cook, so the goods needed to get delivered in time for dinner.

Insisting on a religious education, Naani registered my sister and me as Muslims at school, which required us to attend the Friday Jummah prayer. The Hindu children participated in the temple on the school grounds, and the small minority of Christians used the schoolyard for services on their holy days. The mosque was a make-shift mosque attached to the principal's house across the school yard's unpaved dirt street.

On Fridays, Naani walked the extra two miles up and down hills, nearly one hour away from her home to attend Jummah prayer at the school with us, instead of attending the mosque just four houses away from her home.

Naani also enrolled my sister and me in Sunday Maktab classes or Islamic religious school. My sister never attended. Instead, Salma ran down the road to Aunty Kay's or our cousin's house to play while I attended class. But, Salma never got in trouble because Naani was not the kind of woman who lectured or made you practice by force.

Our Saturday nights were spent in church with my aunt and uncle, who were very active in the small church down the road. It was held at a neighbor's house. Christians were in the minority in our village as most people were Muslims or Hindus.

"Hurry up and get dressed, don't make your aunt late for church," Naani said as she encouraged us to attend church. She also encouraged us to go to the temple when our Hindu neighbors invited us. She didn't think that listening and learning other religions interfered with Islamic teachings. "God is love" was her favorite phrase. She would say, "No religion can threaten your faith as long as you accept that "God is One and God is love."

Naani truly lived by her words. She was married to a Christian, with two Christian children and two sons who did not practice any religion. She was also raising her grandchildren in Islam, yet we all lived in peace and harmony in the same house.

Another rule was to evoke Bismillah's blessing or "in the name of God" before cooking, eating, or giving something to someone. That rule became second nature for me.

One of Naani's neighbors was a single Hindu woman with several children. Some villagers questioned her morals, and she became the gossip of the town. But Naani treated her as one of her own, feeding and caring for her kids like extensions of her own family. Naani's neighbor, on the other side, had lived there with her husband since she was in her teens. He'd since passed away. That's all we knew about Neighboo as she was called. Neighboo was an Afro-Trini, Christian older woman with no children. She was never out and about or talking to anyone, except Naani. They had a ritual every morning. Standing under the mango trees that separated the two houses, Naani shouted, "Morning, Neighboo!"

"Morning, morning," Neighboo replied

"You see meh chicken pass?" Naani asked.

"Yeah, Neighboo, they good." (That meant the chickens were roaming her yard and it was okay.)

"Okay, Neighboo. God is Love," Naani said.

"Praise the Lord," Neighboo replied.

And that was the limit of their interaction except for Naani sharing her baked goodies like pone (cassava pie) or Christmas black fruit cake. Even then, nothing was said. Naani hung a bag filled with goodies on the mango tree that leaned over Neighboo's yard as if the branches were bowing before her as they presented her gifts.

Despite my positive experiences of living at Aunty Kay's and Naani's, my sisters and I were separated from Bobby. Bobby is the eldest and my parents' only son. After Papa's first trip to America in 1969 and for the year while both of my parents lived there, Bobby stayed with Daadi and our uncles up North. And he visited us occasionally down South.

Bobby also moved to America in 1972, but we remained separated. Honestly, it's remarkable that he's still alive today, given the significant health battles he has faced. I'm grateful that American doctors discovered his health issues in time and that he received the care that saved his life. However, due to his extended hospital stays and years in treatment, we didn't reconnect until many years later.

Chapter Four

"We came to America, either ourselves or in the persons of our ancestors. To better the ideals of men, to make them see finer things than they had seen before…." —*Woodrow Wilson*

City of Lights

At the beginning of 1972, my parents returned to Trinidad together. Several days later, we heard that Bobby had made it to America. Of course, Papa had planned everything, but as kids, we weren't told anything. About a week later, around four o'clock in the morning, Mama woke us up one by one, got us dressed and fed, and without ever having the chance to say goodbye to anyone, we were whisked away to the airport.

We weren't told where we were going or what was happening. We only knew to follow my parents' instructions. Though, I had acquired a curiosity about America, particularly Boston. In the few visits my parents made in the two years prior, the name tags on their suitcases read PAN AM. There was a plane logo and Boston plastered all over.

I'd once asked Papa what America was like. He opened our freezer, the non-defrosting kind that had a thick buildup of ice, and he said, "That's what

America looks like." He continued, "But in America, money grows on trees. You shake the tree, and money falls out." I was gullible and felt that I was going someplace magical with money falling from trees. It was exciting even though I didn't know our destination or the immigration process and how it would shape our lives in America.

Buckled down in my seat, which felt more like a waiting room than a plane, I quickly fell asleep. I woke up in a landed plane that felt like it never took off. I'd completely missed the experience of my first flight.

In a flash, we were driving in a car through the streets of New York. It was awe-inspiring to watch all the lights and soak in the enormity of a city. "Pa, look at all the lights!" I said, tugging on him. My father proudly replied, "Every day is Diwali in America."

We got to the hotel, and it was enormous. I thought Aunty Kay's house was big until I entered this giant building, among others, that were even larger and more intimidating. I remember getting inside the hotel elevator. Having never seen one before, I turned to Papa and asked, "This is our room? It's not so big."

Papa wryly smiled and told us, "Close your eyes, and when you open them, the doors will open up to your room." And, magically, when I opened my eyes, there was our room.

Exploring the city the next day, I was overwhelmed with amazement and curiosity. Walking into a grocery store with Mama was like entering a twilight zone. We picked stuff off the shelf and didn't wait for the storekeeper to give it to us. Then, I saw it. *Wow!* I spotted an aisle with books and cards that blew my mind—coloring books with crayons in the next rack—all for me to enjoy. I opened the box of crayons, and the smell of newness made me more excited to color in my book. Proudly walking out of the store with my new book, I thought, *I love America. I hope we never have to go back home.*

This experience shaped my first belief about America: if you want something, you go and get it. You don't have a wait for others to give it to you.

But parading around the city was not so freeing or exciting. Mama held my hands tightly as we walked. "You have to walk on the sidewalk and cross the street only when we reach the crosswalk," she told me as we navigated back to our hotel. It took quite a while for me to figure out the purpose of a traffic light. However, the one thing that I could not figure out to save my life was the old-fashioned radiator. The radiators were shiny and silver, etched with unique designs and motifs, and they were almost as tall as me. *What could it be?* I scrutinized it day after day, finally concluding that it must be where you keep your guns. In the TV show *Bonanza* (One of the handfuls of American shows played on Trinidadian television), they always had rifles, just about the radiators' size. Papa always said, don't touch the radiator; you will get hurt. Yep! That confirmed it; that's where the guns were kept. Needless to say, I was scared shitless, always keeping one eye on it.

By the time we had arrived in America, Daadi, Daada, and Papa's siblings had been in America for a couple of years. They somehow obtained their permanent residence status too. My father was the last to come over, and no one was able to help him. His only way to get a green card was to marry a U.S. citizen. People in the community had married for the green cards and urged my father to do the same. But that meant he would have to divorce Mama, something he absolutely refused to do.

Most of Papa's family lived in Boston except Uncle Ralph, Papa's brother, who lived in Rhode Island. Uncle Ralph had a possible job for Papa. So, in hopes of starting a new life in a less expensive and smaller community, we immediately moved to Providence. Papa didn't think it was a good idea for all the brothers and their families to live so close to one another in case immigration came knocking.

After our move to Providence, Papa and Uncle Ralph become inseparable, working together, hanging out, and confiding in each other. They worked as security guards, while my mother and her sister-in-law worked at the old folks' home. All these jobs were paid in cash under the table.

Nearly a year after we arrived in America, Daada took ill and passed away. This evoked more stress on Papa, who was already trying to navigate life in a new country and culture. His paranoia started to set in after we overstayed our one-year visa. The stress and worry only compounded as he thought about the possibility of getting caught and deported. The pressure and paranoia kept him from thinking clearly. He was angry all the time, and he felt helpless.

Behaving as children do, we weren't making life any easier. It was a difficult change for all of us, but particularly for Papa. He was not used to Mama working outside the home, and he never really had to worry about us until he started living in America. Raising three young daughters was not easy for him in what he considered a wild culture. It was incredibly difficult for him as a young, uneducated man who couldn't thoroughly read and write or drive. He also didn't speak American English. His dark skin and accent were like a sticker across his forehead, labeling him a "foreigner." We were living paycheck to paycheck and constantly moving to stay ahead of deportation.

While my father was traumatized by his immigration fears, I was being traumatized in the classroom. My teacher Mrs. Kerns was a middle-aged tall and slim woman with short strawberry blonde hair. She was always dressed in various colors of polyester pants with a tucked-in shirt and a red blazer. I called her Mrs. Stern for her stern tone. Once I offered to tote her books to the car for her, I got scolded for my improper use of the word.

"No, Jamila, you don't tote the books; you put the books in a tote bag and carry it to the car," she said as she rolled her eyes. In reading class, my pronunciations were always being corrected, much to my dismay. Like the time I spelled zebra with *zed* instead of *zee*. Well, let's just say it left an impression. But the most embarrassing moment came one day when Mrs. Kerns called on me for a simple math question. I was eager to answer, having always been a confident and smart student.

"Michael," she said, "If you have nine oranges, and I gave you one more, how many oranges would you have?"

"Ten," Michael replied.

"Good," shouted Mrs. Kerns with excitement.

"Now, Jamila. If Michael gave six of his oranges to you and four oranges to Kathy, how many oranges would Michael be left with?"

Proudly I shouted, "Nought!" which meant *zero* in British English.

"What are you talking about? If Michael has ten and he gave you six, and he gave Kathy four, what is he left with?" she shouted.

"Nought," I timidly replied.

"Do you understand we are not talking about directions? We are talking about numbers," she said, staring me down in a much calmer but still condescending tone.

For the first time in school, I felt humiliated. I suddenly felt heat rushing from the back of my neck and burning up my face as it tried to escape from my head. The room started to get larger as I shrunk in my seat. I heard the kids laughing, but I didn't understand what they were laughing at or why. I knew nought was the correct answer. *Why was she mad?* I didn't get it, but my psyche did; it got that—*people don't understand when I speak*. And that interpretation plagued me for the rest of my adult life. Not wanting to be laughed at or humiliated again. This incident stopped me from raising my hands or speaking in class. Even class introductions became anxiety-ridden, causing full-blown panic attacks.

My father's fear that immigration was after us became unbearable. He withdrew me from public school and enrolled me in a private Catholic school, hoping to reduce the chances of leaving a paper trail. I didn't care; I was glad to leave Mrs. Kerns behind.

I loved my new school because it was more diverse than the public school. My new friends were mostly Spanish, but there were a few black students too. I was comfortable there. God was part of the curriculum, and my teachers were nuns who loved and encouraged me. I again excelled in school, with mostly As and the occasional B.

Months later, and two weeks before the end of the fifth grade, Papa pulled me out of school for good. His fears had taken over, but his ego couldn't admit it. Instead, he told me, "You don't need to go to school. It will make you too smart, and you will have trouble finding a husband. You already have a dark color. And with your cokey eye, I don't know who would want to marry you."

Papa's instructed me to stay home, take care of Liz, and stay indoors. Salma taught me how to cook, and I developed my own ways of cleaning, running a household, and paying bills by the time I turned twelve. These skills came in handy, and they quickly made me very responsible at the expense of my childhood. But I became known in the family as the strict and responsible one.

Staying home was not enjoyable for me. I really missed school. Foolishly I remained hopeful that Papa would change his mind, and I would return to school. In the meantime, I began my own routine. After doing my chores early, I snuck out of the house every day to go to the library while Papa was at work. I rebelliously checked out books on religions, cultures, and history, and I taught my little sister everything I learned.

I started to become afraid of Papa. He looked so depressed and beaten down. He wasn't singing or telling jokes anymore. Once happy, playful, and funny, my father had become stressed, angry, and violent.

My mother and I tiptoed around Papa's mood. As the baby of the family, Liz was loved by all, but mostly by Papa. She was never scolded or yelled at, and she never got spanked. Salma rarely got in trouble with Papa as he loved her cooking and her love of Indian music and singing. My sisters had commonalities that bonded them with Papa, while I always felt out of place. No one shared in my love and yearning for God, education, or travel. This lack of belonging often made me feel like I was in the wrong family.

Still, I insisted on doing things my way, even if it meant breaking Papa's rules. And that put me in and out of the hospital for the next year. I ended up in the emergency room several times after Papa's beatings, and occasionally from Mama's. However, Mama's licks were due to my lack of cleaning skills. Those beatings resulted in stitches on my fingers from blocking a broom handle aimed at my head.

Even Armando, my father's best friend, didn't raise an eyebrow when my father told him, "If she can't hear, she'll feel." Which meant, if you cannot heed the warnings, then you will pay the consequence. Armando was originally from Sicily and was suspected of having questionable ties to the mob. But for us, he was a funny, short-but-muscular man who spoke with a heavy Italian accent. He called my mother Dolce after he heard papa calling her Doll. And nothing seemed to bother him. Nonetheless, he was the one tasked with carrying me up and down the stairs post-injury when I couldn't walk. He did that for about three months.

Some of my beatings were aimed at my mother. But I threw myself between them, attempting to protect Mama. But most of my punishment stemmed from my defiant behaviors of sneaking out to the library or reading books.

Salma teased me a lot in a typical sister's bickering and annoying way, sometimes by laughing at me when I got licks or when I cried. But the repetition of the behavior wore on my sensitivity; I felt like she was taunting me. She'd say: "Papa hates you. That's why he cut your foot. What's wrong with you? You're not normal. That's why no one likes you." Yet, there were other times when we were inseparable. She would do my hair and make-up and take pictures, pretending that we were movie stars. It was one of our favorite things to do. Sometimes she'd even save her allowance to buy me an Indian record when we made our monthly visit to the Harvard Coop Bookstore in Boston. So, I knew Salma didn't mean the things she said and that sisters fight, which made it even more difficult for me to understand my behavior. I wondered, *What's wrong with me? Why am I so sensitive?*

Fears Become Reality

In the summer of 1975, we made a move to Boston. Once again, we were surrounded by family and cousins within walking distance. My father got a full-time job as a security guard under an alias, and my mother worked as a housekeeper for several wealthy Bostonians. Papa was becoming more social, hanging out with his brothers playing All-Fours on the weekends. Sometimes he gambled at the racetrack, a favorite family pastime.

Things were looking up, and Papa finally let his guard down. He got his driver's license and purchased his first car, a brand-new cobalt blue Chevy Nova, costing about four thousand dollars. I don't know whether he used his real name or an alias, or even what documents he needed to show. But a year later, it was approaching the annual checkup in Rhode Island, which meant a day trip for a complete tune-up at the dealership.

It was a Thursday morning, and we were up early. "Doll, get everybody ready. We have to leave here at eight o'clock. My appointment is at ten," Papa reminded Mama. Nervously, I quietly pleaded with Mama to stay home. I'd convinced her that someone had to stay home to cook and clean up for when they returned.

Little did we know Papa's worst nightmare was about to come true. The dealership in Rhode Island was instructed by immigration to report him when he showed up for his appointment. Immigration had either tracked him down, or someone tipped them off. My father got deported two days later. Mama was given time to stay in the country on bail for another thirty days because she had children. Women with children were given extra time to get everything in order. We stayed for two days with Armando and his wife while Mama calmed down and made her plans. Armando posted the bail for my mother and advised her not to return to Trinidad. He advised her to jump bail and stay while he tried to get my father back to the United States.

Mama took his advice, and within the month, Armando had a beautiful affordable apartment set up for us in Dorchester so that Mama could keep her job. He had people move us from the old apartment to the new one. He also sold the car and used the money as repayment for bail.

Mama confided and told her boss the truth about what happened and her situation. Thankfully, they offered to help. Their daughter hired Salma as a live-in nanny. They trusted my mother and soon gained trust in my sister. Thus, we became part of an extended prominent Jewish family, a relationship that lasted decades.

Puppy Love

The summer of 1975 wasn't all bad. It was the summer I met my first love. He was the boy next door, but what many people might call "trailer trash." Mama was not impressed. She questioned his mother's reputation. He was the second youngest of ten children fathered by different men. My family called him White Boy, but I called him D. Although he didn't know his father, D thought he was part Puerto Rican or Mexican, part Cherokee Indian, and Irish American (from his mom).

D was two years older than me. At first, I didn't even like him. He always wore dirty jeans and worn shoes. The smell of his dogs lingered on him, which I found gross. He was the total opposite of me in many ways. I was always dressed neatly and appropriately, my clothes starched and ironed, elegant, and modest. I wasn't jeans and a T-shirt kind of gal. My long black hair was always clean and brushed. And I was reserved and quiet.

D became friends with my father, whom he affectionately called Mr. White because my father was very dark. However, my mother considered D the dirty little boy from down the street—not a kid to befriend. She scorned him and didn't like him coming inside our house. During the summer months, our trash usually gathered worms. Mama would say, "Call White Boy. He's used to these kinds of things." So, I would call him to take out the trash.

D lived at one corner of the block, and I lived at the other. There was a vacant lot in between where the neighborhood kids gathered to hang out. One day while my parents were at work, D came over to the house with a handful of dandelions. I saw him walking up the stairs, and I greeted him at the front door. He usually came to see Papa. I suspected this visit was to get closer to me.

As I approached him, I said, "My father is not home. He went to work with my mother." And as I attempted to walk away, he gently grabbed my hand and said, "I've come to see you." Then he handed me the dandelions. Being very shy and respectful so as not to be rude, I smiled and thanked him. He stayed around, and we chatted for a while.

Two days later, it was a Friday afternoon after Jummah prayer, which I prayed in secrecy. Standing out on the back porch, my hair was still slightly wet from my ritual shower. A warm, gentle breeze flowed through my long black hair. I felt peaceful and beautiful, as I usually did after praying, especially on Fridays.

Suddenly the most loving pair of arms was placed gently around my neck as a warm body pressed against my back. It made my heart drop and sent shivers down my spine. I smelled him. That smell I had come to detest suddenly became magically fragrant. D slowly turned me around and looked into my eyes so deeply it made my entire body shake.

I was spellbound by his blue eyes. He caressed my face with one finger while his other hand ran through my hair. He didn't take his eyes off mine, not even for a second. He then slowly pulled me toward him and kissed me. It was my first kiss.

I was so lost in his presence—lost in his eyes. He pulled me closer and closer. We both held each other until our arms became numb. I was so scared and nervous and almost ashamed to look at him. Finally, after what seemed like hours, we pulled away, and he tried to kiss me again. He softly pulled my chin up with his hand, and as my eyes caught his, I began to cry. I couldn't help it. I wasn't even sure why I was crying. It all just felt so…raw.

That infamous day my parents had driven to Rhode Island to get the car serviced, I had stayed behind to cook. D came over and spent the day helping me do my chores. We talked the entire day about our future. "I'm going to marry you one day," he kept saying, making me more shy but hopeful.

D had a beautiful fair complexion with a gold tint matching his golden blonde hair and complimenting his deep blue sexy eyes. When he looked at me with his mesmerizing eyes, it was as if I were the only one in the room. His piercing eyes made me quiver like a frightened child. He became much more than puppy love—he became my archetype. D defined how love should feel: exciting, nerve-racking, passionate, intimate, romantic, safe, and accepting. These feelings became my benchmarks for love. I'll know it was true love if those feelings existed.

D made me smile from deep within my soul. A spark ignited something inside me when I caught him sneaking glances at me. He was the kind of guy who would make someone do a double-take. I felt fortunate because, aside from the physical attraction, his aura was calm and easygoing, and that attracted me like a moth to a flame.

Chapter Five

"As with the butterfly, adversity is necessary to build character in people." —*Joseph B. Wirthlin*

Breaking the Rules

Six months after Papa got deported, he returned to America. His outlook had changed. He no longer wanted to stay in America permanently. His new goal was to work, save money, and return to Trinidad, where he would build his big house and live happily. His dream seemed so simple, yet so far out of reach.

Before coming to the United States, Papa owned two plots of land. It was given as a wedding present to my parents. One was down South, which he sold to buy our visas and tickets for our migration to America. The other was up North.

Upon his return and while working as a security guard in Brookline, Papa befriended an older wealthy widower. She was a Hungarian woman named Mrs. Tate. My father had the gift of gab, and Mrs. Tate owned a forty-unit apartment complex in Brookline, a very expensive and safe Jewish town. She was smitten with my father and offered him an apartment rent-free in exchange for taking care of the property. That included collecting rent, calling the plumbers or electricians if needed, and taking out the trash weekly.

The apartment was a gorgeous three-bedroom, one-bath home on the first floor with a wrap-around porch. It was walking distance to the library, cultural centers, and public transportation, which I'd learned to ride while my Papa was in Trinidad. I still wasn't allowed to go to school, though Brookline high school was practically in our backyard. And the move separated me from D., but I was still excited to live there.

Our family lived there for almost four years—the longest we'd stayed in one place. We'd cut ties with my father's family since my father firmly believed that one of his brothers reported him to immigration. Brookline was a safe place, a prestigious town. We weren't likely to bump into Trinidadians or other islanders.

My parents continued their full-time jobs and cared for the building in the evenings. I became the bookkeeper, collecting the monthly rent and calling the maintenance personnel.

Papa bought his second car in cash, a used Chevy Impala. It was mint green with tan leather seats and a bench seat in the front. Having a car meant freedom, which I saw Papa enjoying a little more than he used to. We often took road trips to visit Papa's childhood friends in New York. The beatings were reduced to the occasional slap or threats of being belted. But the emotional abuse was far from over. It had become more a way of life—a standard way of speech that I'd become accustomed to.

I was allowed to spend nights with my sister Salma at her live-in job in Newton, an adjacent town even more affluent than Brookline. While my sister was living there and only coming home on weekends, I was left to care for the house, cook, clean, and take care of Liz and the building while my parents worked.

Mrs. Tate spent a lot of time with us. She lived in India in her earlier years and loved to practice her Hindi with Papa. Although he kept telling her we weren't from India, she insisted we were. And Mama enjoyed taking care of her too. Mrs. Tate was a welcome addition to our lonely home. She also enjoyed an occasional glass of wine, so an exception was made in our household for Manischewitz kosher wine. Mama made good use of it too. She used it to make Trinidad fruit cake at Christmas: using wine and Hennessy to soak the dried fruits for a year; she then used the fruits the following Christmas. She also kept brandy to rub her joints and to soak Papa's head when his migraines were terrible.

Life was getting better overall. But I couldn't understand why an uncomfortable feeling always hovered over me like a dark cloud. They were feelings of not belonging, of being a misfit, and somehow different. Hidden inside me were feelings of not being good enough and of being unloved. Leaving an absolute emptiness, like a dark hole, I kept covering up inside me, thinking it was normal to feel this way. But the pain persisted, and I would often cry myself to sleep.

Trying to feel normal and useful, I got a part-time job. My job was to help the elderly neighbors with their chores. I also babysat for the next-door neighbor and helped around the Jewish holidays. The smell of challah bread, matzo ball soup, and pickled fish filled the neighbor's kitchen on Hanukkah. Jewish families were very particular about their holiday table. My neighbor taught me to polish silverware and set an elegant table. She also showed me how to entertain in style, with proper table manners and social skills. Sometimes I attended her religious holiday to help serve and somehow ended up mingling with the guests and hanging out with the kids my age. And I managed to earn a few dollars along the way.

I felt more comfortable and accepted by outsiders than within my family. My inner quest for God strengthened in that community as I was introduced to a new religion—Judaism. I was often invited to take part in Seder dinner or to sit shiva if someone passed away. Sometimes I even attended the temple on the Sabbath with the neighbors. The Jewish stories are very similar to those of Islam and Christianity. The prophets of the Bible were the same prophets in Islam and those that I found in Judaism. It quenched my thirst to learn about different cultures and religions.

With my father's permission, my sister and I enrolled in swimming classes at the YMCA and disco lessons at Arthur Murray's dance studio, which led to a new passion. I discovered my love for dancing. And soon, I bartered my babysitting services to indulge my fantasy. I studied and performed a classical Indian dance called Bharatanatyam, with the prestigious, renowned dancer Neena Gulati. I'd finally found a new joy.

One of the perks of living in Brookline and having wealthy employers was that we got to wear hand-me-down designer clothes. Salma's employer was the buyer for an exclusive and expensive department store in Boston. We were introduced to Gucci, Versace, and other brand names. At fifteen, my first handbag was a Gucci purse with a matching wallet, which I cherished, even though I had no idea who or what a Gucci was. Her employer was kind to us. She loved that I was ultra-skinny and tall. She thought I was beautiful, so she'd send all sorts of designer clothes for us.

During the day, I'd sneak out to the library to continue learning and checking out books on geography, sociology, and religion. I also worked on math and science at the library. Pushing the boundaries, I enrolled in finishing school at the Academy Moderne, owned by Mildred Albert, a television fashion personality and director of the Hart modeling agency. I kept it a secret from Papa. Some girls in the neighborhood were going, and I wanted to go too. I'd saved enough money to go to modeling and finishing school, giving my family more reason to make fun of me. They laughed and taunted me, "Oh look, Cokey Eye wants to model." They followed me around, mocking me, closing one eye, pretending to model.

The feelings of never being celebrated for my accomplishments or supported in my endeavors ought to have deterred me, but it didn't. After graduating from finishing school, I joined the Hart modeling agency, where I landed a local modeling job as a foot model. Later, I landed gigs for a Bacardi ad and a poster ad for Barnes and Noble's bookstore.

But nothing boosted my self-confidence. If anything, it made me feel more insecure and even more out of place. As I continued working for Hart, I was eventually tasked with dressing models between their walks. I would show up backstage to help dress them, shocked by men and women being naked in the same room! The champagne toasts and hookups after the shows made me very uncomfortable. I knew the modeling world was not for me.

My father seemed happier and a little more relaxed with money coming in from Mama and my sister. With their combined incomes and no rent to pay, the finances were okay. My pocket money was enough for me, so I didn't get an allowance. My sisters got an allowance after the bills got paid, and any extra cash was banked in Trinidad in case Papa got deported again.

One August evening in 1979, my father and I were taking out the trash from the units. I was walking up the stairs to the second floor behind my father when he stopped, stumbled against the wall, and grabbed his chest, crying out, "Ouch! Shit! Oh, shit!"

"Pa, what's wrong?!" I asked.

"Nothing," he answered.

"Let's keep going. How much more?" he continued.

"Let's go home. Mama will come and help me," I insisted.

We arrived home, and he asked me to rub his head with his favorite Trini remedy, limacol, as he collapsed in his green rocking chair. "Doll, make me a cup of coffee and get me two Excedrin," he called out to Mama. Papa had always suffered from terrible migraines, and the only medication available to him without insurance was Excedrin. Ten minutes went by, and I noticed that my father was becoming sleepy, almost limp. The fear of immigration made Mama afraid to call the ambulance.

My heart was beating faster and faster, knowing something wasn't right. Unafraid of Papa at that point, I took the responsibility and dialed the operator.

"I think my father is having a heart attack."

Taking Chances

Papa was unable to take care of the apartment, and his doctor suggested no heavy lifting; that meant we had to move. We only had Mama and Salma's income to rely on, and with our move came rent. Eventually, we moved back to Dorchester, where rent was more affordable. There was also family support and where I was only five blocks from D. He and I were unable to stay in touch and hadn't seen each other in about four years.

It was tough seeing Papa walked through the door with Mama's help. He had just been released after weeks in the hospital. Papa no longer looked like a man who could chase me around the house. He could barely walk; his face was chiseled and beaten down by time and depression. He was frail as he'd shed close to eighty pounds. Seemingly spiritless, it was as if old age and illness were getting the better of him. He appeared dazed as he'd awkwardly looked up at an angle, unable to hold up his head. His clothes grew more ragged and oversized as if he'd gave in to passing time and not concerned about his appearance. His voice trembled when he said, "Eee-ye." My heart knew at that moment that he'd given up.

The next week, deciding to take a chance, I made an appointment to talk with the guidance counselor at Saint Gregory's, an all-girls Catholic high school. When the day arrived, I met a tall and slender older woman in her mid-sixties with short blonde hair. She wore an angelic smile, and I immediately trusted her.

She introduced herself as Sister Katherine. "What can I do for you, dear?" She invited me to her small office at the back of the building. It overlooked the nearby brook. I was comfortable in her office and somehow felt protected, perhaps because of the enormous crucifix above her desk looking over everything or the sizeable praying hand bookends on her bookshelves. Somehow, I mustered the courage to tell her the truth. I had no legal papers, no school records, and a five-year gap in school. My only wish was to enroll for the school year as if it were so easy.

It was a sucker punch to my gut when she said, "You may not be able to return to school. I mean, you've missed so many years, and the school year has already begun." I buried my head in my hands as my light when dim. In shock, I was unable to cry or to feel any emotion. I was numb and shaken up.

"Oh no, dear," as she leaned over to hug me. "Now, now."

My lips begin to tremble.

"You see, dear, I'm not sure where to put you. I'm not sure what grade you belong in," she said, shaking her head. "Let's get you something to eat," getting me up to walk me to the cafeteria.

On the way, she explained that I could take a placement test, which would guide her to where I belong. "Perhaps you would be better taking a GED rather than completing high school," she explained. She treated me to a grilled cheese sandwich before she left to speak to the principal. Returning about half an hour later, she told me that I could take the test when I felt ready.

"How about now?" I shouted with excitement.

"Well, dear, you might want to study. It's an important test," she replied.

The truth was that I didn't know what or how to study for it. I was just so excited that I agreed to take it the same day.

Two days later, I got a phone call from Sister Katherine, asking me to return to the school. Worried and concerned that they had reported me to immigration, I nervously approached the office. My heart was pounding, beads of sweat formed on my forehead and neck. Luckily my parent's names or addresses were not on the application, so the school didn't know where I lived.

It's okay, I repeated as I gently hugged myself. The principal and Sister Katherine were coming from the rectory as we crossed paths before reaching the office. "Hello, dear!" exclaimed Sister Katherine as she hugged me.

I smiled with a sigh of relief. *She looks happy to see me.*

"Hi," I waved sheepishly.

"Sister, this is Jamila, our little genius I was telling you about," Sister Katherine said as she introduced me to the principal. "You're such a beautiful young lady," replied the principal, smiling as she gently placed her hand around my shoulder to escort me into the office.

As we sat down, Sister Katherine was all smiles. "Well, Jamila, I'm not sure how this happened, but you passed into the eleventh grade with ninth-grade math. How did you do that?"

Exhaling while closing my eyes, tiny drops crept out of my eyes, one after another. It quickly turned into cascading tears that drenched my shirt. In some odd way, a feeling of vindication came over me. Years of sneaking off to the library had paid off. I was going to high school. Thou, I was no longer a confident student, but at least I was a student. And that meant the world to me.

I was convinced that once I finished high school, that dark, painful hole inside me would begin to disappear, and I would be normal.

It was our first Christmas since Papa had come home from the hospital. D was also home for the holidays. He'd been at Marine boot camp. I begged Mama to invite him over for Christmas dinner. She finally relented.

We didn't do Christmas trees and didn't usually get Christmas presents. But that year, Papa had a gift for all of us. Eagerly ripping the paper off, I could hardly control my excitement. Finally, I unwrapped it only to find a used tube of Bengay, a pain relief ointment. My heart sunk with disappointment, and internally I began to cry. Saddened, embarrassed, and disappointed, it felt like Papa had put his hands in my chest and ripped my heart out. I ran out of the room and secretly cried for quite some time. I vowed never to accept another gift.

Later in the day, D came over, and we all sat around the dinner table, elegantly set with our fanciest plates and glasses. Nervously, D came and sat beside me, holding my hand beneath the table. As we began to eat, I whispered, "Bismillah." It must have been said louder than usual because it irritated Papa. My praying was no longer a secret. My father began to insult me, "Look, look. Big Muslim wants to pray." The beratement continued, ending with "why does this Cokey Eye have to sit here?" Unable to hold it in anymore and dying of embarrassment, I ran out of the room sobbing yet again. Under my breath, I murmured, "I wish you were dead."

While trying to calm me down, D proposed to me. He said he would finish basic training in the spring and would be back to marry me and take me away. We would move to the Marine compound in North Carolina, where military families lived. The thought of being with him calmed me down and gave me something to look forward to. But Christmas became a day I hated and dreaded with a passion.

We rang in a new decade that New Year's Eve, 1980. And ten days later, on a Thursday morning just before eight, Mama had left for work an hour prior. Liz was enrolled at the public school within walking distance from our house. She and her friends left about half an hour earlier for school. For the first time, I was running late. The phone rang, which was surprising and irritating as I was rushing out the door. A moment of hesitation told me to race back to the phone in case it was D calling.

"Hello," I said.

"Hello, this is the doctor from the hospital. Is your mom home?"

"No, she went to work. This is her daughter. Can I take a message?"

"Is there any way to reach your mother?"

"No, she's working at several homes today. I'm not sure which one. Is something wrong? Can I take a message for her?"

"How old are you?"

"I just turned seventeen."

"Okay, you're old enough. Your father passed away this morning from another heart attack which occurred…."

Quietly falling back on my bed, I tried to comprehend what I'd just heard. Still in shock and unable to cry, I couldn't keep up with the thoughts racing through my mind. *Wow, he's only forty-seven. That's too young.* Then I realized I was home alone. *What if he came to haunt me?*

Being a coward, I shook nervously as I called my youngest aunt. I tried to remain calm as I took action. I knew Mama would rely on me—I was the responsible one. After notifying my aunt, I hailed a taxi to Mama's job in the city to deliver the news in person.

I sat in the taxi, trying to figure out how to break the news to Mama. *What would life be like without Papa?* A fear came over me, but it was different than before. It wasn't a fear of Papa beating me, but a fear that I'd be haunted. Then I thought about my more significant fear of how we were going to make it. *Would we be okay without him?* Overwhelmed with sadness, I regretted spending all that time fearing him.

By the time Mama and I got to the hospital, most of the family was there crowding the hallways. You could hear the wailing as we approached the room. Mama, still unsure what she was allowed to share, leaned on her sister-in-law's shoulder and let out a big sigh. It had been about three years since we last saw the family. As more family piled into the room, excitement grew with my anticipation that maybe my cousins would come too. Finally, I spotted two cousins in the corridor. We ran toward each other. "Oh, my God!" We hugged and cried.

The weeks and months that followed my father's death were the worst of my life. I became more frightened and scared of Papa despite him being gone. I was convinced he would come back to haunt me for wishing him dead. The guilt was killing me. I never fell asleep, dreading the darkness of the night with memories of him lurking around me.

One night I nearly died out of fright. Mama and I were sleeping in her room at the back of the house. The same room that Papa had spent his last couple of days. My sister was back at her job. Although Liz was the youngest, she was extremely brave and slept alone in the large front bedroom. Whoever was sleeping with me had to touch me or throw their legs on me so I could feel them next to me all night. Mama did just that as she fell asleep.

Restless and unable to sleep, I was lying on my right side, staring down the spooky and lonely hallway leading to the living room. Peeking out of the living room was Papa's green rocking chair. As my eyes shifted to it, the chair started to rock. I laid frozen, unable to scream or turn toward Mama. I shut my eyes tightly, trying to ignore what I just saw. Seconds later, I felt a scratch across my foot. *It must be Mama's toenails. At least she's awake.* I sighed.

"Ma, ma," I whimpered.

"Hmm, what?" she says, still asleep.

"Can you hug me? I'm scared."

I asked while grabbing her arms, securing them around me. I was still scared but feeling a little safer as the sleepiness started to set in. Seconds later, the blanket tucked up to my chin started to pull away from me. I pulled it up and tried to fall back to sleep. Again, the blanket began to slide off. Again, I pulled it up, snuggled in, and tried to go back to sleep. The blanket again slid off me as if it were being pulled. Slightly irritated, I quickly turned around, ready to yell, "Stop pulling–" And as I did, I saw a hand pulling the blanket off me toward the ceiling. The blanket was levitating high above the bed. I screamed the loudest scream, and, in a flash, the blanket dropped toward the bed.

"MAAAMAAA!" I screamed, crying and shaking, unable to move. Mama panicked and quickly turned on the lights.

"Don't leave me alone! Don't leave me! Stay here! I'm scared," I screamed. I hurriedly repeated verses of the Quran I didn't even know that I knew. Every prayer that I knew—Christian, Muslim, Hindu—I blurted out.

Fortunately for me, I had met a Muslim boy at Papa's funeral. His family came from the mosque to read the Quran and perform the ritual funeral prayer. His family performed religious rites for those who did not know how to do it. They were very well respected in our community. But we'd met once before at a Moulood Mama had when Papa first became sick the year earlier. At the funeral, he and his cousins were hanging out with D, and I learned that they were high school friends. We had all become friends, even while D went back to the Marines. My new friend and I had much more in common, though it wasn't the crazy attraction and calmness I felt with D.

That night, Mama instinctively called him. It seemed like only minutes, and he was there. She explained what happened, and he came, hugged me, and started to read the Quran until the sun came up.

The next couple of months got even worst and the most terrifying of my life. Scared stiff after that encounter, I could not sleep. I was convinced that Papa was haunting me; I refused to be alone, not even for a second. Mama or Liz had to go to the bathroom with me. They showered with me. They slept with me, holding me all night but to no avail. Mama even flooded the living room with wall-to-wall mattresses making room for friends and family to spend the night with us. My new and only Muslim friend took me to several religious men hoping to rid me of evil spirits. One of the holy men, well-known in the community for this sort of thing, made a tabeegh for me to wear. It was a prayer wrapped in a cloth and pinned on me as a repellent against evil spirits.

I pinned it to my nightgown and tried to fall asleep. The next day, the pin was still fastened to my gown, but the prayer was gone. We searched everywhere for it, but it was nowhere to be found. Returning to the religious man for another one, he said, "Your faith is weak, and you are not a believer. That's why the prayer left you."

His words inflicted a deep sadness within me, and I used it to affirm that I was a bad person. It was true that I did not know enough about Islam to believe that a talisman would work. But to hear that I was not a believer created more doubts, and I became even more frightened. Three weeks went by with no sleep, and I started to get severe headaches. It was the beginning of my battle with migraines.

Finally, my friend decided to take me to his father. His father was the sincerest Muslim I had ever met. He performed Jhare (a religious sort of exorcism) over me. Still, I could not sleep. I'm not sure which was more terrifying—the fact that Papa was haunting me or that I was not a true believer.

One evening, to get out of the house, I decided to visit my Haitian friend from school. While sitting on her couch waiting for her to make me a cup of tea, my worn-down body and mushy mind were so exhausted that I finally fell into a deep sleep. I slept all through the night until midafternoon the next day.

The following year was graduation, and I was beaming with excitement. All my friends were filling out college applications and getting ready to leave home. I, too, had filled out my college application. I had big dreams of becoming a doctor. I wasn't sure what kind of medicine I wanted to study, but I loved the sciences. I excelled in chemistry, biology, and physics. Papa was no longer holding me back. And my life was mine, free to live it as I wished, or so I thought.

One evening I came home from hanging out with my Haitian girlfriend. My oldest aunt was in the kitchen with Mama waiting for me. "People are talking, and it doesn't look good for a young girl to be running around with a boy," she scolded as she talked about my Muslim friend. Then, carried on for a bit, with Mama sitting there, not saying a word. Finally, my aunt said, "You're going to get married. No more talk about school."

I had never talked back to anyone, especially to an elder. But she was messing with my dreams. Perhaps that is what fueled me to want to lash out, but I didn't dare. Instead, I kept it in and stifled my dream.

D and I had broken up after I refused his marriage proposal. As much as I loved him, my life was not with him. I knew there would be no opportunity for school or religion. I wasn't ready to have children as he'd insisted on having right away. And I doubted that he would stay away from pork and beer.

While all my friends were busy moving into their dorms that September, I was getting engaged to be married the following year. Having no choice in the matter, it was either my Muslim friend or my father's friend. The friend we visited a lot in New York, and he was the same age as Papa. He had asked for my hand in marriage, promising to take care of me as he was older and financially stable.

But I knew that if I were going to marry anyone, it would be my Muslim friend. Ever since that night, he stayed up and read the Quran for me; I felt he was holy, and his faith would protect me. He was already in college and a practicing Muslim. I knew I could learn a lot from him. So, I chose what I craved the most—a spiritual life with a loving family.

We were married in a traditional Islamic wedding in 1982. Uncle Mageed, my favorite and only remaining Muslim uncle, gave me away, taking my father's place.

Chapter Six

"Love one another, but make not a bond of love ... stand together yet not too near together ... [for] the oak tree and the cypress grow not in each other's shadow." —*from Kahlil Gibran's poem, "On Marriage."*

A Wholesome Life

My husband and I moved into our first apartment, modern and beautiful as I imagined it would be. It was on the third floor of a Boston triple-decker home. His sister owned the house, and the family occupied the first and second floors. Our living room turned into a master bedroom, offered more space. It was situated near the front of the house, giving us perfect views of the road where our brand-new white Dodge Charger was parked.

Our apartment was cozy, clean, and warm. Family surrounded us, so there was no need to lock the front door. We simply waltzed into each other's apartment at will. Soon after we moved in, one Friday night, his cousins called, "Hey, let's go to the midnight movie!" And my husband turned and asked me if I wanted to go. Then it hit me—for the first time in my life, I didn't have to ask permission. I didn't have to make up excuses or plead and fight to go out. I could do whatever I wanted, and I loved it. I didn't want to waste the opportunity to work hard and strive for a better life.

The first two years of marriage were hectic. I worked as a bank teller for the Boston Five Cents Savings Bank and tried to be a super wife. I woke up early to make breakfast and always prepared our dinner. Despite all the work, it was enjoyable always to be surrounded by his large family. The air was filled with laughter and playfulness instead of yelling and arguments. Lightness rather than heaviness. It was a new way of living, and I found it strange yet refreshing.

We seemed to be on a two-year plan for significant milestones. Two years after we got married, we bought our first home on Friday, July 13. People called us ambitious, and perhaps my husband was. But for me, it was one more attempt to prove that I was good enough. I felt that having a house at my young age would make me feel good, and it would fill up that hole inside me that had robbed me of my joy.

The house was in Ashmont Hills, which was considered the better side of Dorchester. It was a beautiful old colonial house converted from a single into a three-family home. The house was gorgeous; it had lots of old charm with a grand oak staircase, high ceilings throughout, and gleaming hardwood floors. You could easily imagine the grandeur this house claimed in its glory days.

We lived on the second floor while working hard to restore the house and make it a home. The family again joined us in the new house, occupying the first and third floors. Our doors remained unlocked.

I smile, remembering the ease and comfort of our living arrangements. "Jay, whatcha cooking, girl?" my girlfriend asked as she casually waltzed her way in. We chatted for a bit, then she reminded me of her hospitality, "Jay, don't cook on Saturday. I'm making a pot of soup. All-yuh come and eat. Nah."

We were all welcomed as family in each other's homes. I felt contented. This new freedom of working, taking care of the house, and spending time with family made me happy and hopeful that the emptiness inside me would soon go away.

We continued working on our beautiful house for the next two years while I worked and attended college part-time. That was my only real experience attending a public, co-ed school, and it was terrific. I quickly made friends with a small group of classmates.

I was thrilled to have friends that weren't family, even if they were friends I could only see at school. To be wise about my education, I enrolled in a computer science program because it was a money-making field in technology's emerging world. My classes were in Fortran, Pascal, and calculus.

What was I thinking?! I had no business taking those courses, especially since I didn't have any interest in learning about computers. I yearned to study religion, cultures, biology, and other sciences, yet I doubted the practical job opportunities. But my guilt won over. I couldn't stand the idea of spending my husband's money on a wasteful degree. So, I switched to business and finance as a part-time student.

For the first time, school wasn't so much fun. I'd shut down my learning brain and lost interest in going to classes. My old insecurities were creeping back in. I felt stupid, and my confidence took a hit. I was embarrassed and afraid to tell my husband that I failed my classes because he would then realize how stupid I really was. Echoes of *you're good-for-nothing,* and *you're so stupid* played loudly in my mind. I wondered why my husband married me what did he see in me. Many beautiful and smart girls would have jumped at the opportunity to marry him. I started to wonder what was wrong with him for choosing me.

I've always wanted two children. It felt like two would make it more affordable to give them a great life. My husband and I had talked about starting a family when he finished school, when we had a house, and when we felt financially stable. After he finished school, nothing was stopping us, and it seemed to start a family was the next step in building our lives.

The thought of having children excited me because I knew for sure that children would make me feel worthy and good enough. I knew that I would always have someone to love me. I imagined that my children would be as smart as their father. He excelled both academically and in the workplace, so I knew they would have a bright future. I also imagined that my children would be faithful practicing Muslims and develop a love for Islam and God. I could not imagine a better person to be the father of my children.

Ever since the night my husband had stayed up all night reading the Quran for me, I knew that he had all the qualities I wanted for my children—his unshaken faith, good looks, and intelligence. I was proud that my children would be born from good family stock. Although my husband was social and kind,

I found his mannerisms to be harried. He moved at a fast pace, reminding me of my father. It caused the same anxiety that I had felt years earlier when Papa was around. Unknowingly, I was transferring my unresolved feelings for my father onto my husband.

Nonetheless, the hope for a brighter future outweighed any doubts. Nothing was stopping us from starting a family. And I knew with all my heart that a child would fill that growing dark hole in a way the house or school didn't.

A Prince and A Princess

Months into trying to conceive, I became pregnant but suffered a miscarriage nine weeks later. My doctor told me it was normal and that many women experienced miscarriages through no fault of their own. But my unhealthy mind was convinced that I didn't deserve a child and that God was punishing me. I suffered in silence, convinced that I was a bad and undeserving person. I knew that I was so bad that even my own parents didn't love me; at least, that's what my inner thoughts reaffirmed for me every chance they got. The miscarriage made me yearn for children even more. But I also knew deep down that I didn't deserve them. Fear was always lurking in the background—a fear of turning into my father.

A year later, I was given a second chance when I became pregnant again. School was put on hold, so my focus could be on my health. I cut out sweets and medication like Excedrin for my now recurring migraines. I was determined to be extra careful during that pregnancy and took better care of myself.

For thirty-six hours, I labored without any medication, not even a muscle relaxer per the request of my husband. He did not believe in drugs and did not want any traces of drug in their system. I endured the worst physical pain imaginable, yet it was all worth it. We were blessed with our little princess. Princess Laila.

After one of my favorite Indian movies called Laila Majnu, a Bollywood version of Romeo and Juliet, I named her Laila. Looking down as the doctors pulled her out with her curly lips and bronze skin, I was immediately enchanted. In Islam, one of the most powerful nights in Ramadan is called Laila-ul-Qadr. It's the night all of the angels, ready to forgive sins, are sent to earth looking for those in prayer. As I saw my baby, I knew that was her—the miraculous and powerful beauty of the night.

Never has a man been more in love with his child than Laila's father. If I was important to him, our daughter knocked me off that pedestal. The two formed a unique bond. The kind where, even in her infancy, you could see her admiration for him and his undying adoration for her. I didn't even mind that my daughter did not want to breastfeed or would rush to him instead of me for comfort. I felt safe that my husband was there, assuring me that any sort of abuse would not be tolerated.

A peaceful joy came over me as I watched them together. It was the kind of father-and-daughter love every girl ought to experience. I knew my daughter would know she was loved.

A new addition to the family meant a new house. Two months later, on Halloween, we moved into a single-family home in the suburbs and rented out our home in Ashmont Hills. I became a stay-at-home mom, caring for our family, our home, and our investments. My previous knowledge about caring for a building came in handy, so I took care of our Ashmont tenants' needs, even going to court when needed, daughter in tow.

The closer I became with my in-laws, the further I drifted away from my own family. Our daughter was the catalyst that brought us back together, even if it was superficial. Mama loved Laila from the day she was born. She adored her and spent as much time with her as possible, walking three miles daily as she made her way from her house to ours to play with her granddaughter. My sisters rallied around her, too. My brother became sober, giving up drugs and alcohol, which had become a way of life for him as it managed his pain. And for a while, life was tolerable, even joyful, within my family.

Laila was so easy to take care of. She hardly ever cried. She was always laughing and was just a barrel of sunshine. We wanted another child so that Laila would have some company. Three and a half years and a twenty-eight-hour delivery later (again without medication), we welcomed our precious Prince Omar Aziz. His delivery was different; whereas his sister was whisked away as she was a jaundiced baby, the doctor immediately placed my son on my stomach. I was taken back; *wow,* looking down at my baby, I was in awe: his soft, warm skin was slimy on my bare stomach. Thou, his tiny eyes were closed, his head moved around with opened mouth looking to suckle. I can't explain it; it was as if I knew him. I felt like he was mine, like he needed me as much as I needed him; it was an instant bond. As the nurses took him away, I was pleading that *"my baby's hungry, and I need to feed him."*

I named him after the Imam of the mosque who had since passed. His middle name was an ode to his grandfather. Both men were devout and influential in my religious life, and I hoped that my son would follow their religious path.

On my second day in the hospital, the nurse came in while I was asleep and laid my precious baby next to me. It must have been time for breastfeeding, as he wiggled his way to me and started eating away, waking me in the process. The nurse then came over to check on me. We both smiled.

"May I take a picture?" she asked. "This is the most adorable thing I've seen." And as his sister gravitated toward her dad, so did my son toward me. He became my zen baby. He was happy chilling on my chest, playing with others from afar. As long as I was within my baby's view, he was fine, and I loved it. I felt needed with a purpose.

At Omar's three-month follow-up, the pediatrician remarked, "He's amazing. Does he ever cry? He's so chilled" "yea, he's my zen baby, " I teased. She commented on his contentment and my calmness with him, asking about my daily routine. I shared:

As soon as he woke up in the morning around eight, I changed his diaper, then fed him followed by a cool bath. After his morning bath, he was treated to a massage. His diaper was changed often during the day, usually as soon as he awoke from his naps. We spent a lot of time playing together, even while I did my housework. Before bedtime, he got a warm bath followed by a relaxing massage.

"Ah, you're setting his internal clock with the warm and cool baths," interrupted his pediatrician. "Babies learn that the cool water is daytime, and the warm represents nighttime. The massages are a great way to stimulate his circulatory system. He's content because you spend so much time with him and incorporate him into your daily chores. He doesn't feel the need to compete for attention."

Yes, I was always paying attention to both of them, thou, Omie needed me more. The children were precisely three years and six months apart, which worked out great. As Laila when to half-day pre-school, Omie and I had our "together time." I would strap him in his baby strap on my chest, facing him outwards to watch the action. I picked up, cleaned, did laundry, and vacuumed, all the while he's secured on my chest. Omie's favorite was making the beds, his little chubby feet daggling out the strap. The more excited he got, the faster his feet wiggled. I would throw the sheet up in the air as he gasped, almost holding his breath, waiting for the sheet to fall on us, then he'll burst into uncontrollable giggles.

Fridays were a special day. It was the day they were allowed to eat the candy given to them during the week. Every day they would ask, "is today Candy Day, mom?"

"No, Sugars. It's two more wake-ups."

However, when Friday arrived, they were beside themselves. "It's Friday. Do you know what that means?" I'd say as I woke them up.

After breakfast, I'd put all the candy on the floor on top of a sheet, put the TV on, and let them go to town. I kept them in my view as I prepared for the rest of the day. The kids ate candy to their heart's content. In reality, how much candy can one really eat in one sitting? After about two mini chocolate bars for Laila and a gummy bear bag for Omar, they were full.

"Are you sure you had enough?" I would teasingly ask, reminding them they could have as much as they wanted.

"My tummy hurts. I'm so full," replied Laila. Omie held on to his bag as he was a slow eater and ate only gummy bears earning him my nickname Sugar Bear. Then off they went for a bath before we got dolled up for Mosque, ending the day at Mama's house. It was our Friday ritual.

A Blessed Life

Those were the most treasured years of my life—being at home with my two children, whom I loved and adored. My son brought me a different kind of joy, where I felt needed—his whole body wiggled as his hand stretched out towards me, murmuring, "Mum, mum, mum": his reaction was priceless and lit up my day. We were spending more time with my mother and sister since the children were born. My sisters started family night. Every Friday, my sister Salma and her husband and my family would gather at my mother and Liz's house for dinner. It gave them a chance to play with the children. With more girls in our family, my sisters welcomed and adored our first baby boy.

We couldn't manage to make plans on Saturday night, because that was Salma's special, romantic evening to spend with her husband. They had been married for five years, had no children, and they spent every day together. *Why did they need a special Saturday night?* I didn't understand. But I did wonder what kind of love they had; how nice it was that they were so into each other. I especially envied the way they joked around and laughed with each other. Salma didn't have to ask his permission to do anything. She would say, "Hey, honey, I'm going with the girls to the beach tomorrow; you could come if you want." And that was it. We had different lives, and mine had become more structured.

Ramadan was one of those structured events. It's our holy month of fasting, and it has become one of my favorite times of the year. There are lots of rituals and a lot of time spent socializing with family and the community. With each passing year, I prayed that I would be happy. Ramadan is the month where if you prayed sincerely enough, whatever you wanted would be granted. It's the month where Muslims try their best to strictly practice the faith, and I was no exception. I made a special effort to be extra good in that month, each year, hoping that the darkness would turn to light.

A typical day in Ramadan began at the break of dawn with breakfast called Suhoor. After breakfast is the first prayer of the day known as Fajr. At the beginning of the prayer, we make our intention to fast. It is not allowed to eat or drink or engage in sexual activities until the sun sets, and you break your fast. We (my husband and I) broke our fast with family or in the congregation. The feast is called Iftar, and it is customary to break-fast with milk and dates, following the ways of Prophet Muhammed.

The Prophet broke his fast with a glass of milk (probably yogurt) to aid in digestion, and a palm date, to symbolize the Prophet Moses, who found strength in the palm date after forty days in the wilderness. After breaking the fast, it is time to pray. Before praying, one must purify themselves getting ready to approach God. There are some prayers you recite in your mind while performing the purification ritual known as Wudu.

Wudu starts by doing everything thrice and using your right hand to wash. You start with your mouth, rinsing three times to wash away anything bad that you may have said since your last purification. Then you rinse your nose for anything bad you may have smelled. Next is your eyes for anything bad you may have seen. Then you pass your wet hands over your head to wash away bad thoughts you might have had. Next, you wash your ears for anything bad you may have heard. Then your feet up to your ankle for anything bad you may have stepped on. Finally, you wash your hands, left first, up to your elbows for anything bad you may have touched.

The coming-of-age men took turns leading the prayer and are lovingly corrected by an elder. Children are never hit or talked down to as I found out it's un-Islamic to hit your kids, particularly your daughter.

After dinner is Taraweeh, the nightly prayer read-only during Ramadan, the Quran has thirty chapters. One chapter of the Quran is read each night. And so, at the end of the thirty days of Ramadan, you have completed the recitation of the Quran.

Hosting an Iftar dinner was an event I looked forward to. I felt honored to cook my best dishes for our fasting community. Members of the community playfully fought for nights to host the Iftar dinner, as they are granted an added blessing for "feeding a fasting person." It's mostly a chance to socialize with family and friends, making the month more enjoyable.

These functions kept us connected to the community and the religion. Being part of this ritual brought absolute peace and calmness even though the month was filled with hectic activities. Knowing that the fasting person cannot get mad or their fast would be broken made me feel at ease. People were more friendly and generous, not just with their money but also with their time.

The night before Eid were incredibly fun and hectic. Everyone was bustling around getting fitted for their new outfits and preparing for the fun-filled day ahead. The day starts with early morning prayer at the mosque, followed by socializing with community members and their families, then gathering at the family's house to spend the rest of the day, eating, laughing, and playing cards. Food was plentiful and served all day for anyone passing by.

Eid, weddings, and other holidays were excuses for huge family gatherings. We spent our time talking, enjoying music, eating good food, and playing All-Fours.

It's enjoyable watching our children playing with their cousins or talking with others. Alcohol, smoking, or other vices were never part of our events.

On all accounts, life was pretty good. And during Ramadan, I felt safe and connected to God. I was taught that Satan got locked up, and the angels were roaming the earth, and only good things happen in Ramadan. If you died during Ramadan, you would go straight to Jannah (heaven) because it's a blessed month.

Ramadan made me feel safe. But as soon as the month was over, I felt spiritually unprotected. And I became fearful that bad things could happen. I was always waiting for the other shoe to drop.

Chapter Seven

"If you are trying to be normal, you will never know how amazing you can be." —*Maya Angelou*

What's Wrong with Me?

I had managed to carve out a perfect life even if it was crafted based on outside pressures from family, culture, and society. It felt like I had what I'd imagined a happy life to look like. Yet even when I had it, I still felt dead inside.

I found myself repeatedly searching for answers. *What would make me deeply happy?* I'd thought it was marrying well, or the houses, or children, or financial stability. But they all provided only a temporary high.

Society made me believe that who I was just wasn't enough. There were unspoken pressures to improve me all the time. To become skinnier, more beautiful, more wealthy, more successful, more involved. My response to these messages was to drive myself relentlessly to be the best wife and mother, but I forgot myself in the process.

One area where I had control was in keeping a spotless house. Having kids and white carpets weren't very practical, yet I insisted on having it to prove that I was good enough. My children were well mannered and always clean and fed. If we had guests over for dinner, I went out of my way to set an elegant table in a spotless house and serve a delicious meal. *This all proves I'm a great mother and wife, right?*

In reality, no one has ever pressured me into being perfect. It's been self-imposed. My unresolved feelings for Papa were never dealt with, and I transferred those feelings to my husband. I looked toward my husband for my happiness, and when I wasn't happy, I blamed him. It felt like everyone was doing things to me, so it was never my fault.

Through no fault of his own, my husband replaced my father as an authority figure. He became someone I needed to take permission from, someone to answer to, and someone to be feared. Seeing his car pull up in the driveway created a certain anxiousness in me. I could be myself during the day, but I had to be on good behavior when he was home.

We were not equal partners. I didn't even know what an equal partner was. I didn't take the time to get to know my husband; I just kept treating him as my father. I wanted everything to run smoothly and be happy, but I didn't even know what happiness was or what it should look like. I kept telling myself it would look like my life. Yet I still always wondered, *Why don't I feel happy?* That dark hole had become a fixture in my heart and seemed to be growing exponentially.

I became increasingly sensitive to the slightest of criticism, and everything took on a different meaning. If my husband told me the food was too spicy, I took it as a personal criticism. It felt like I was good-for-nothing and couldn't even cook. It made me feel like an inadequate wife if he was looking for a particular shirt in the wash or the ironing basket.

I even questioned my abilities to be a good mother and friend. But there was no real evidence to support such claims.

If my guests were late, I took it personally. Internally, I compared the scenarios. *They weren't late for so-and-so's dinner, but they're late for mine. They must not like me as much.*

I also become overly critical of others, judging other people's houses' cleanliness or thinking their tables weren't set as pretty as mine. The list of criticisms went on and on. It felt better for a short moment. But it created my false sense of pride to put down others to feel better about myself. The thing is—it didn't work. It only made me hate myself more.

With the criticisms piling on top of my insecurities, I deepened my hatred for myself and for being different. I felt guilty for not being satisfied or content. And for being critical and judgmental. The negativity swirled, and I picked internal fights with people I had no reason to fight with. Everything and anything that was ever said to me, especially growing up, was interpreted as something "they did to me." A constant pointing of the finger and blaming everyone else.

At ten in the evening, my favorite late-night show came on. While Laila and dad went to sleep, it was the perfect time for me to unwind and breastfeed my baby boy. Rocking him, I would look down at his angelic face, talking and smiling with him while he breastfed; sometimes, his eyes would catch mine, and he would stop feeding and smile, looking right at me. It made me laugh deep down inside as I knew my baby understood me. I prayed that he would grow up to know how much I loved him.

Even though my baby fell asleep, I kept him with me as I watched the show about two married couples: one with two infants and the other couple who wasn't sure about having kids. They and all their friends are around thirty-something. The star couple of the show have the kids, and the wife is a stay-at-home mom. The husband worked in advertising. They just bought their first home, a fixer-upper. I was always envious of their relationship and the way they talked about issues like equal partners. They laughed together, and he never complained, though the house was always a mess. There was always laundry that had to get done and a sink full of dishes. But he never complained, and he complimented her on working so hard at home.

When I compared myself to the wife, the commonalities stopped with our roles as housewives and mother of two kids. My house was always clean and well kept, spotless even. Dinner was on the table every night, and clothes were cleaned and ironed. She and her husband always ended their disagreements with, "I love you; we'll figure it out."

Does this kind of relationship even exist?

I could not imagine what it would feel like to pull up in the driveway and have a sense of relief when seeing my husband's car. In one episode, the star wife had a bad day at the supermarket with the kids. She scolded one of them after her youngest threw a temper tantrum. She lost her temper and ended up yelling at her son in public. She was relieved when she came home and saw her husband's car in the driveway, knowing he was home, and he would comfort her, not blame or call her names for having a bad day.

Would I ever get to experience love? Real romantic and passionate love? Is there such a thing? Would I ever have a partner who's my friend that I enjoy talking to? Would I ever not be afraid of getting yelled at for making a mistake? There were many times I simply lied instead of admitting to my mistakes, just to avoid being scolded.

I wasn't unhappy with my marriage or with my life and children. They were the ones that brought me any sliver of joy. I was unhappy with myself. Thoughts of running away plagued me, but I didn't know where I'd run to. *Where is there a place that would take away this immense sadness?*

Thoughts of suicide started to pop up again. I knew I couldn't do it. I knew it would not work because the option had failed me in my earlier years. I had taken a bottle of Bayer aspirin one night after a beating from my father, but nothing happened. I ended up with an annoying ringing in my ear and painful stomach cramps, the kind that makes you keel over and beg for mercy. But that was it.

My doctor diagnosed me with postpartum depression. But I knew it wasn't that. I'd had these feelings most of my life, though they were at peak intensity by then.

On many happy occasions, like gatherings we hosted at our house, we were having fun, people were mingling, and nothing out of the ordinary happened. But on one particular Saturday, I found myself sitting on the porch, feeling incredibly lonely. Like I didn't belong.

How can I have these feelings in my own house? And where did it come from all of a sudden?

I somehow managed to excuse myself, and I found a quiet place to cry. An overwhelming sadness washed over me, and I wasn't even sure why. My heart told me that there was something wrong with me and I couldn't be happy. Or that I didn't deserve happiness. There wasn't anyone to talk to, and even if there were, I didn't know how to explain my unhappiness. The few times I tried, my sadness was met with: "What do you have to be sad about? Do you know how many girls would kill to be in your position?" Or as a Trini would say: "Your ass is too fat; you have nothing to worry about" or "If you had real work to do, you wouldn't have time for this nonsense."

No one understood how I felt. Not even me. My father had been dead for years. There was no more abuse, no more beatings, no more name-calling.

Instead, it was replaced with a loving husband, family, and children—a home filled with God's love and the financial freedom we had planned. My children were the loves of my life. I had everything anyone can ask for and more.

Why? Why can't I be happy? What the hell is wrong with me?

Living this miserable existence, I became convinced that I was doomed to live this way because it was what I deserved. It's said that "time heals all wounds." But in some relationships, time only makes the wounds deeper.

We were outgrowing our three-bedroom, one-bathroom ranch style home. Rather than buying another home, my husband decided to build our forever home.

As our forever home got closer to completion, instead of feeling excited, it felt like the noose tightening around my neck. I felt like I was being buried alive, brick by brick, screaming but no one can hear me. We moved into our new 3500 square feet home surrounded by in-laws (six to be exact) living side by side. This beautiful four-bedroom, three-bath home filled with grandeur was transforming into my private prison.

Thirty years into the odyssey of self-loathing, I believed that loneliness and sadness were my best friends. I thought I deserved a horrible life of instability and all the hysterics of shame and guilt. All this threw me further into isolation and deeper into self-hatred. Those thoughts were enough to blast me into the stratosphere, where I promptly began to plummet to earth. At terminal velocity, every circuit in my body misfired. The fall was endless, yet the giant earth came rushing toward me.

My behavior became erratic. The better my life got, the nicer people were towards me, and the more my husband showered me with gifts, the deeper I fell into the cave of despair.

This perfect life couldn't be real. Why do I deserve it? Thus, unknowingly, my behavior sent me on a path to do everything possible to sabotage it, including a one-night stand. It was suffocating and fearful, waiting for the other shoe to drop.

And drop it did.

Divorce had never entered my mind, yet there I was. My actions had brought me in front of a judge and into a custody battle—a two-year-long battle with no support system and not a foot to stand on. I didn't want the house or money. I agreed to walk away quietly like a mouse, leaving everything behind—including my children.

Convinced that I was incapable of caring for the children, having no money, no job, no degree, and no support system, I was a total mess. I didn't want to risk the chance of becoming abusive and inadvertently hurting my children. And I didn't want to drag my children around, moving from here to there. My heart knew my children were better off with their dad and his family. They had love and God, stability, and a belief in education, especially for girls. But my heart also knew that it would kill and destroy my husband if I took the children away. I didn't want to hurt him more than I already had. He did not do anything wrong to deserve this situation. His only crime was marrying me, a damaged, mentally unstable girl.

My children did not deserve this either. I felt sorry for them for getting me as a mother. I wished I could be different and normal like their aunts. And I questioned why God would do this to them.

Months of sleepless nights followed, very reminiscent of my earlier days. I spent nights endlessly pleading with God to show me a way to show me what to do. I reminded him that He was there with me in the operating room years earlier. *Please, show up for me again.*

As I weighed my options and tried to figure out what was best for my children, I immersed myself in prayer and worship. I finally took myself out of the equation and focused on my children's lives. I made a list of all the things I wanted for them, and next to it, I wrote who could provide that for them. The answers all pointed to their father. Even though my soon to be ex-husband was angry and wanted to punish me, he was a good and loving father.

And I knew the biggest and best gift I could ever give my children was a religious foundation. My wish for them was to be with their cousins playing in the cul-de-sac, in the home that their father built. I wanted them to taste the sweetness of Ramadan. And I wanted them to have a good relationship with the family and have an excellent secular education.

The list was all the things I was unable to provide. In essence, I needed to trade my earthly happiness for their everlasting spiritual happiness. And this led me to make the most significant yet most loving sacrifice of my life. I decided to end the custody battle in my children's best interest, giving their dad physical custody.

It became apparent to me that staying in that house, in that life, I would have cruised along in the same fog I'd been in for decades if I lasted that long. I was an empty shell, a pitiful existence rather than a functional human being. I came to believe that my psychotic breakdown, which led to my reckless one-night stand, helped save my life. Not just my pulse, but my capacity to become.

Chapter Eight

"In order to save myself, I must first destroy the me I was told to be." —*The Dreamer*

Finding My Power

For the first time in my life, I found myself alone. I'd gone from my mother's bed straight to my husband's. There were so many things I'd never done, like sleeping alone, going to the cinema by myself, or eating at a table for one in a restaurant. And there were even more things I wanted to do, like finish school and travel the world.

But I was thirty-two and divorced, with no education, money, or skill set. Having no place to live, I ended up living with my mother. She always nagged me about finding a place and seemed to enjoy blaming me for how much I'd messed up my life. Living in that eternal shame was draining.

Others were scared for me and eager to point out all the reasons that I ought to be scared. Yet I wasn't. I felt free. For the first time in my life, there was no one to answer to. No one to justify my actions too. Finally, I was able to be myself, mistakes and all. The age of reckoning had arrived.

I found a job and moved into my own place. Those first few days of being by myself in my apartment were liberating. I'd made it my own by decorating with my choice of colors, putting books on the shelves, and hanging pictures on my walls. It was indeed mine; I picked out and paid for everything with my own money. Walking around the few rooms, I wondered what to do next.

But the novelty quickly wore off. With no one moving around me, no friend to talk to, no children to hug and snuggle up with, I didn't know what to do with myself. The life I had once assumed was idyllic—the one with a husband, children, a house, and family—had vanished. Here I was, facing my new future, alone.

Being alone can be a blessing and a curse. I had an appreciation for the freedom that I didn't know I'd craved. But I missed my children, my old routine, and structure. In an attempt to distract myself, I made plans for the future, putting a lot of effort at work, and tried to get on with my life. But the exhausting effect of my thoughts was inescapable. I spent more time than I wished I had with my only two real friends—depression and self-doubt. It seemed that those two had been lurking in the background for years, and they finally had permission to come out and play. They were the ones that never left my side, not even for a moment.

On a Wednesday mid-June afternoon in 1996, I was on my way to Harvard Square to check out a potential college when a deep sadness and self-loathing took over me. In truth, it had been stirring since the day I called the college. Those feelings of not being good enough, emotions of failure, and the feelings that people were laughing at me were suffocating. Struggling to catch my breath, I sat on a bench along the Charles River, contemplating jumping into it. I felt unable to pull myself out of it; thoughts of suicide flashed in my mind, leaving me paralyzed. I sat there for hours until the sun began to set.

The next morning, I decided to seek help. Determined that I had only one job, and that was to heal myself, I bought every self-help book I could find. The Oprah show became my new best friend. And I found a therapist. Not an easy task coming from a generation and a culture that frowns upon airing your dirty laundry.

My therapist was a licensed social worker who shared an office with her husband, a licensed psychologist. After the first session, which was an intake, she concluded that my brother sexually molested me.

The therapist said, "I found that you have suffered severe physical, emotional, and sexual trauma and—"

"Wait!" I jumped in. "Physical and emotional abuse from my father, but he never sexually abused me."

"Not your father. Your brother sexually abused you," she whispered.

"What?" I asked in disbelief as I glared into her eyes. "How did you come up with that?"

"Well, you said your brother slept in the same bed as you, and he's five years older. He's the one who took you to the bathroom in the night, not your sisters or your mother. I believe that's why you are behaving promiscuously...." She said everything as if she were reading from a textbook.

Adjusting myself in the chair getting ready to leave, I calmly said, "You obviously don't know about my culture. My brother is the oldest, and it was his duty to take us to the outhouse outside the home and not safe for girls. And he sometimes slept in the same bed because all the kids shared wall-to-wall mattresses."

I walked out of the office, rolling my eyes and shaking my head at her incompetence. But still, within earshot of the therapist, I mumbled under my breath, "Do you even know that I grew up poor in a third world country?"

She quickly replied, "Yes, I know you're from India."

I didn't bother to correct her, and that was my only experience seeking counseling. I've since learned that it's crucial to find a therapist who understands your culture, religion, and society.

There I was again, without formal therapy to help me. So, I clung to my faith. Even that proved challenging at times as I was an outcast in the community. Friends of the family started dropping off one by one. But only after they'd said their piece, blaming me for actions that they knew nothing about or accusing me of not loving my children. Others said I was stupid for not taking any assets from the divorce. I also became the center of gossip among many members of my mosque community.

One member approached me one night after Taraweeh prayer and asked me why I bothered coming to the mosque. But I held fast, "I am going to the mosque for God, not anyone else." At one fundraising dinner, I sat alone at a table set for ten. My religious community had become judgmental, unforgiving, and unkind. If this was Islam, then I wanted nothing to do with it. There were many times thoughts of leaving my religion crossed my mind.

I also desperately needed to make money, and my only work experience was with the bank and personal experience with mortgages. I decided to focus on what I had rather than what I lacked. So, I returned to the bank and landed a job.

My first job came from a mortgage company that hired me as a processor's assistant. Initially, my job was to copy and stack files according to the investor's requirements. I threw myself into it, and in two short months, I became a processor. And one year after that, General Electric recruited me as a mortgage underwriter.

Eventually, I ended up as the underwriting manager for another large mortgage company. That new position allowed me some financial freedom. It afforded me to travel, but it also afforded me to pay child support. Even so, I had little bills and was able to save money slowly.

Despite all the progress, I still experienced deep sadness. That dark hole, though shrinking, was still large enough to evoke self-doubt, and it did so often. I spent many sleepless nights yearning for my children. I replayed my life repeatedly, asking what I could have done differently, racking my brain trying to figure out what was wrong with me and how I could fix it. Preoccupied with what people were saying about me, I wondered if I was any better off now than when I was married.

On the weekends I didn't have my children, I sought refuge in New York nightclubs. It became my form of therapy. I'd grab a friend, drive to New York, meet up with some more friends, and party all weekend. And as fun as it was, it only masked the pain. It did not fill that dark hole.

Fed up with me and with the negative feelings, I grew weary of the same old story. My apologies for the same mistake over and over never resulted in even a hint of forgiveness. I was ridden with shame. Shame for not only what I did, but also shame for who I was.

Despite these challenges, my skeptical mind was reaffirmed, and I found it challenging to seek help. I knew with all my heart that no one would understand my feelings. No one had the same deep reservoir of pain that crippled my life. I was different, and I hated myself for it.

Then one fortuitous day, a friend introduced me to transformational learning.

"Transformational learning," I said. "What's that? I'm not interested in school right now. I want to find out why can't I be happy."

"Then this is the place for you. But it's hard to describe," my friend explained. "You have to experience it by being open and embracing a new way of being, and it will create a paradigm shift for you and transform your life."

I understood none of what she was saying, but I was so fed up with feeling and living the way I was that I enrolled in the seminar she suggested. I didn't have anything to lose. If I really didn't like it, I could leave within the first hour and get a full refund, no questions asked.

The first day at the seminar, I plopped down into my front-row seat, already pissed that I'd spent money that I did not have for something I knew would not work. It was 7:55 a.m., and the workshop was about to begin. I impatiently waited for the speaker to start so I could just get everything over with.

Promptly, at eight o'clock, the speaker, Richard, walked on stage to greet everyone with an enthusiastic "good morning, good morning. Welcome, hello, hello" as he looked out into the audience. And then Richard noticed a young man making his way to his seat.

Richard called out to him, "Good morning! Welcome! What time is it?"

The young man replied after looking at the big digital clock on the wall. "Hi, it's three minutes past eight o'clock." Then he proceeded to take his seat.

"What time did the workshop start?" asked Richard.

"Now. It starts at eight o'clock," replied the guy in a nonchalant way.

"When you signed up for the workshop, what time did you say you would be here?" Richard continued.

"Uh, eight o'clock," the guy answered with a puzzling tone as if to say what's the big deal.

"But you arrived at three after eight," Richard replied as his eyes zoomed into the guy as if no one else was in the room but the two of them.

"Yeah, but I made it on time. It took a little time to find my name tag, and now I'm here." The young man proceeded to defend his position as we all waited for the interrogation to end. This went on for half an hour. You could sense the frustration in the audience.

We were all rolling our eyes, watching the clock, and shaking our heads. *What the hell did I get myself into? I didn't pay all this money to watch someone get picked on for being seconds late.*

And just when I'd had enough and was about to get up and walk out, Richard said, "I know you guys are thinking. When does the seminar start? I want you to know; it started at eight o'clock."

We all looked at each other with furrowed brows, puzzled at his audacity.

"You guys just got a lesson on making excuses," Richard stated. "You see, in life, we come up with lots of reasons for not doing what we say we're going to do." He continued, "These reasons look legitimate and appear real. Yet they're still excuses. You see, if you—what's your name?" as he looked to the young man he'd pestered.

"Tom," said the young man.

"Okay, Tom. If you were going to receive a million dollars by being in your seat by eight o'clock. Would you have shown up at three after eight and still expect to receive it?" Richard asked in a very non-shaming way. "Or would you have made sure you were in your seat at eight o'clock?"

Tom replied, "Are you kidding? I would have been here at seven-thirty!" He laughed along with the audience.

"That's right!" Richard shouted. "If it were valuable to you, you would make sure you were on time. So, this could be a three-hundred-dollar seminar, or a three-thousand-dollar seminar, or a three-million-dollar seminar. This is about your life; what value do you put on that" Richard asked.

Then Richard had my attention.

"I'm going to tell you that wherever you are in life, you're there by choice," Richard said.

My internal voice started to scream. *That's not true. I did not choose this shit; you don't know anything about my life.*

And almost as if Richard could read my mind, he said, "You may not have chosen your situation, but you have the choice to change it if it's not working for you." Richard continued with a small exercise on insights.

"I want you to be aware of how many times you say 'Yeah, but…' when you are talking about your situation. Yeah, I know what you're saying, but…."

The audience all giggled, half nervously, as we knew exactly what he was talking about. Excuse-making was a recognizable trait for all of us.

Richard's insights made me aware of all the times I'd made excuses. Yeah, but! was my usual way of speech that I was unaware of. "Yeah, I know, but you don't understand." During my divorce, I constantly talked about going back to school—it was the first thing I wanted. When friends asked me about my future plans, I would say I would like to travel and go back to school. They supportively offered me programs to look into and ways I could make that happen. I would reply, "Yeah, I wish I could do that, but I have to work, and I have bills to pay Plus, all my free time is for my children." And I continued that story for a long time. And Richard's phrase of "keeping your word" meant that if you say you're going to do something, you do it, no excuses.

This new way of thinking changed my life forever. I was a master at making excuses for everything until that day. "Saying what you mean and meaning what you say" became my favorite phrase. If I say I will be somewhere at 8 a.m., I will be there at 8 a.m. No more excuses.

It occurred to me that I complained a lot without wanting to change. Or maybe I didn't want to do the work to change.

Awareness is key to transformation because it forces you to live in the present moment, to notice and pay attention to who you are being in that moment.

This new awareness created a paradigm shift that enabled me to see things clearly. I'd so desperately needed to look at my life from a different angle, but I hadn't known how. It challenged my imposed belief that I was too busy and too poor to follow my dreams. I had to face the truth about who I was being. No longer was life blurred with fog. The fog had been lifted, and I could see clearly for the first time. And I saw that I had choices.

It was like stepping out of black and white life and into a technicolor one. And it started to show up in my everyday life. One time I was arguing with the kids to clean up their room. I'd asked but to no avail, then I started to yell and made it about them, saying how messy they were. I had read somewhere that parents dealt with this all the time. The solution was to close the door and respect their space. But that didn't sit well with me. It was still my house, and I wanted it clean. It irritated me to walk past it, so I kept yelling for them to clean it up.

I got on the phone with my friend and said, "I just want peace. No yelling. I just want them to do what they're told." And as I was saying it, I heard myself. I became aware of what I was saying and what I was doing. The two didn't match up. It was an ah-ha moment that made me giggle. I was saying I didn't want yelling, but I was the only one yelling. I said I wanted peace, but I wasn't being peaceful. Instead, I was verbally attacking my children, saying they were messy, and bullying them into doing as they were told. Immediately after the call, I went over and hugged them, put on some music, and said, "Let's take care of our stuff and put away our clothes." We sang and danced while cleaning up. It was a revelation—things could be peaceful and happy along the way, just the way I'd wanted.

Is This the Truth or My Interpretation?

Awareness is the key. I kept that motto at the forefront as I continued with my transformational learning. I felt that I'd lived so much of my life in a daze, not paying attention to who I was being and what I was doing. I wasn't even aware that my actions impacted not only me but also everyone around me.

I needed to put my life in perspective and make sense of it. That's what we do as logical human beings. We add meaning to everything to try to make sense of things.

When we have an experience, our psyche tries to make sense of the incident by attaching our feelings or misguided logic to the experience.

This happened in fourth grade when Mrs. Kerns yelled at me. I took it to mean she didn't like me, which was how I felt. My narrative became: "My teacher doesn't like me because she always yells at me." And then I lived as if that were genuine and real.

Let's say you become convinced that someone's action means something, and even though you have no proof, you know with certainty that's what they meant. And no one could convince you otherwise. Has that ever happened to you?

When someone tries to offer a counterpoint, you say, "You don't understand. She hates me." Any possible resolution is met with "Yeah, but...." That means, *Yeah, I know what you're saying, but I don't really want to change the way I'm feeling. I just want to complain.*

I joined a transformational workshop at Landmark Education that encouraged me to revisit my childhood and reexamine the facts of what happened. I needed to see if I was stuck in my interpretations of my experiences. I decided to rethink every narrative that made me feel unloved, not good enough, or unworthy. It was like rearranging a puzzle.

Until then, nothing had given me hope of getting rid of my dark hole. I felt like I was doomed to a life of misery. I tried medication for depression, but it just left me groggy and confused. Medication promised to pull me out of the dark hole. But that implied the dark hole still existed. And if it still existed, then I could fall back into it. Thus, medication was only a temporary fix.

Transformation taught me to reframe and create a different meaning for my experiences, which empowered me instead of dragging me down. I had to make a different narrative, one crafted with love and compassion to flood that dark hole with an abundance of light. Flooding the hole with light pushed everything to the surface so I could deal with it. I could look at it, forgive it, and file it away.

The hole disappears with this process. That once dark, empty, and lonely hole now shines bright with light, love, and all things good. Shame, guilt, humiliation, and other PTSD symptoms thrive in the darkness but cannot survive in the light.

Through my studies, I came to understand that behind anger is pain. That meant pain is the feeling, and anger is the behavior. Acting out your anger is an unhealthy way of releasing the pain that can build up. What's worse is that angry behaviors don't solve the problem. To solve the problem, we must recognize where the pain is coming from. Often, when we get mad and have an angry outburst, it has nothing to do with the person we're taking it out on. We are reacting from a place of buried pain.

This was the case with my father. Indeed a warm drink with no ice was not the kind of thing that made someone so angry that they would carelessly risk hurting or hospitalizing their own child. Instead, it was his buried pain that he released through anger. A healthy-minded person uses positive means such as meditation, exercise, vigorous workouts, or talk therapy to release that energy. But that wasn't the case with my father; he didn't know how to handle or control his anger.

I'd learned to separate the experience of getting my foot cut from my feelings about the incident, and it created a new approach to the problem. My story was that Papa didn't like me; he hated me, and he tried to chop my foot off. This interpretation is filled with pain because of the meaning that I attached to it.

In other words, the meaning I'd attached to that incident was more devasting, and it lingered in my mind recking havoc at every turn. THAT created the dark hole. It wasn't the actual cutting of my ankle, but what I thought that event represented. The meaning that I had assigned for all those years was that my father didn't love me. And it hurt. My transformed version was that Papa was a hurt man who didn't know how to control his anger. It had nothing to do with me.

And this discovery freed me! All these years, I thought he did this or that to me because he hated me. I discovered that, in reality, he hated himself.

I can now see my father in a different light, as a hurt man who had a difficult life. He did the best he knew, and I can have compassion and empathy for what he went through. I'm no longer afraid of him, and I wish he were still here.

Transforming my stories to have loving backdrops and knowing that I am and always was loved made all the pieces of the puzzle fall into place. Those loving backdrops also helped me to think more positively and not jump to opposing interpretations. Logically speaking, when we feel loved, it is easier to give love. The practice of loving myself formed a habit. It is now more manageable for me to be aware of when I'm going down the path of Self-Hate.

When an event happened, my new approach was to create a new way of thinking, one that empowered me rather than stopped me from taking action.

As I became more self-aware, I noticed that my negative self-talk stopped me from making good decisions. This negative self-talk created negative thinking, which led to negative actions. I call it Self-Hate Irrational Thinking, or SHIT.

SHIT doesn't care what I feel, intend, or wish—it will not waver. If I'm late for an appointment, fretting and yelling won't help me arrive any earlier. If I am having a bad day, taking it out on others won't change my Self-Hate or my Irrational Thinking. That only makes the SHIT worse. If I lost my job and got upset, would it bring my job back? Or did my SHIT make it worse for me to find another? You see, my SHIT doesn't care that I'm upset. It does not care that I'm hurting myself or others. My SHIT makes me entitled to stink up the place. It's up to me to clean it up.

There's also nothing right or wrong about my SHIT as it's open to different interpretations. The interpretation is never accurate, yet we carry on as if it's real. Again, your SHIT doesn't care if you're happy. You can never make the best choice when you let your SHIT make the decisions. It will only bring you more SHIT. So, stop SHIT-ing all over yourself.

Self-Hating Irrational Thinking had been around since I was a teenager. We all have it. It's the voice in your head that always seems to be talking. You know the voice that won't shut up. Like when I made a mistake, and I yelled, "I'm so stupid." Pay attention to that voice inside your head. It's very influential. Thirty years of playing the same old tape and all it did was fuel my insecurities. I knew I had to change the tape.

If you don't record new messages, the voices will keep playing long after the abuse is over. It was eye-opening to realize that the negative voices in my head are not reality. I retrained myself to look at what actually happened and not my feelings about it.

For instance, another narrative that plagues most women, including myself, is the feeling of "I'm not good enough, and something is wrong with me." As long as I feel shitty about myself and think that I am the problem, nothing will change, and no growth would occur. Taking responsibility by stopping the victim role, changing the tape, and staying true to my word, I knew I had a chance to boost my happiness.

I'd learned to center myself by sticking to the facts and not focusing on my feelings about whatever was happening. By challenging the negative chatter (You're too poor to travel, blah, blah, blah), I kept myself out of my SHIT. I asked myself if the chatter was helping me to move forward. Did it empower me or light me up? The answer was NO. So, I gave it up because I knew where it would lead me—right down SHIT's creek.

Challenging your beliefs is the foundation of transformation. It's how you create a paradigm shift. It's also how you create an empowered life that will bring you harmony, grace, and balance.

One summer, I attended a party with my cousins who told me (gossiped) about some of the people attending the party. I was told that a group of people didn't like me. When I asked why no reason was given. One cousin said, "I think they are jealous of you." Of course, I didn't want to go after hearing that. I knew I would walk into the room and feel uncomfortable because they'd be talking about me behind my back. And it would change my attitude and affect how I related to them. At most, I would only want to say a friendly hello then be on my way. I wouldn't enjoy the experience because I couldn't be myself.

But I was transforming and needed to find a better way to handle these situations. I sat down to look at the facts. The only fact I had was that my cousins overheard them talking, but I didn't hear it. It was hearsay or gossip. Refusing to deal with gossip, I decided to BE myself. I imagined that everyone in the room loved and adored me and that they could hardly wait to see me.

I became excited and happy to see them with a massive smile on my face as I walked into the room.

"Hi," I shouted with excitement, and my arms stretched out, ready to greet everyone. "It's so nice to see you. You look great as always," I said while hugging and laughing as I made my way around the room. I gave out compliments like "look at my beautiful family," and "I missed you guys so much." The entire atmosphere changed to be friendly and enjoyable. People were engaged with me, talking, and laughing, which almost validated my compliments. I realized that I am responsible for the energy I bring into my space.

The minute I started to think *they don't like me*, I immediately recognized it as my Self-Hate Irrational Thinking, and I changed it to *what if they love me?* And I become loving again. I become my true self. I came to understand that my presence contains energy, and it's my responsibility to emanate positive energy.

Chapter Nine

"Out of suffering have emerged the strongest souls; the
most massive characters are seared with scars."
—*Kahlil Gibran*

Clarity, Change, and Transformation

This chapter is a brief interlude to explain the steps of transformational
thinking. It has helped me immensely in my recovery from the drastic and
subtle effects of PTSD. I know it will help you too. Yet, this is not a substitution
for seeking therapy for your specific needs.

The first step in recovering from any abuse is recognizing that it took place
and getting clear about what happened.

Part of my ongoing transformation was to look at the areas of my life where
I had negative stories. I started to reexamine that fateful July evening in 1973.
Usually, I would tell the story that my father hated me, and he tried to chop
my foot off for reading. Since the incident was never talked about, I was left to
believe whatever I wanted. And for years, I thought that Papa had chopped my
foot with his machete. That's the way I interpreted that event, and the constant
taunting from my sister embedded that thinking into my psyche.

All of that collapsed to create that hole inside me. It formed my narrative and became the truth in my mind. Living with the reality that my father hated me caused me to hate myself. Hating myself meant that I was constantly telling myself I was not good enough to be love, and asking myself why anyone would love me. Hating myself also meant I didn't deserve to be happy because I was not loveable; it affected my self-esteem and confidence. When I stopped listening to what others said, and separated my feelings from the facts, did things become clear. Then I could see the event for what it was.

Papa threw the mug; it hit the wall, bounced off, and cut my ankle in the process. That's it! That's all that happened. Those are the facts. Everything else was my Irrational Thinking and a made-up story. In other words, the event was done. It's not still happening, but the story I've attached to the event lingered, growing over time until it consumed me.

This ongoing reexamination of my traumatic life events led to real transformation. The transformation awakened my empathetic and compassionate side. I was able to see my father as a man who was fearful of life, not someone to fear. He had fears about immigration, raising daughters in a different culture, providing financially for his family, and caring properly for his children. The more he buried the anger and guilt, the more it consumed him. And it affected his health, ending his life at forty-seven.

The truth is, I will never know precisely why Papa was angry. No one knows but Papa. Perhaps even he didn't know. My newly found compassion led me to forgiveness. I didn't think I needed to forgive him for many years because I was never mad at him for throwing the cup. I didn't realize it at the time, but I was angry at him for not loving me.

Separating my stories from the facts clearly showed me the way forward. I made up the story that he didn't love me based on how he treated me. But upon reflection, I realized that his anger, and all the other things that were consuming him, had nothing to do with me. If Mama or Salma were the ones who handed him the hot soda, they would have been the ones who suffered a severely cut ankle. I wasn't his target; I just happened to be there. Papa was fighting his own demons.

My breakdown that led to my divorce had nothing to do with my husband, children or family. It had to do with me and my demons. This understanding brought me to a place of forgiveness. Forgiveness for my father, mother, sister, and everyone who contributed to my trauma. And probably most importantly, I forgave myself for all the self-hating and for blaming others for not loving me.

In reality, I was the one who was causing my misery. So, I took accountability for it. And that freed me from the blame game.

It took time and practice for my new way of thinking to feel comfortable. The more I practiced, the more it became second nature. Does practice make perfect? Maybe. But I prefer to believe practice forms habits. I had practiced hating myself, and it turned into a habit. Now I practice (and will continue to practice) loving myself. That will turn into a habit too.

The second step to recovering from abuse is committing to change. I was so fed up with my old un-empowering story and desperately wanted to change it. I was committed to change at all cost. I've found that when I wanted to change, I listened and took action. But when I didn't really want to work for the change, I complained.

Growing up, I was tall and skinny, but I had gained weight after my children's birth. People made fun of my weight. Part of it was cultural, but being teased about your weight eventually wears on you. I complained that I was getting fat and needed to diet. But I really didn't want to do the work of exercising and eating healthier. So, I made excuses like I didn't have time to exercise or didn't have the money to join a gym. There were affordable solutions, like walking or jogging in my backyard or around my neighborhood. These are great alternatives, but did I do it? No way! But it didn't stop me from complaining about it. Then one of my friends told me, "Stop your whining. You look great, but if you are unhappy, then do something about it. It's no fun listening to a complainer." And she was right. I took action, did the work, and dropped thirty pounds that summer. Remember that you should only lose weight for yourself and your health, not from societal or peer pressure. The most important thing is that you commit to the change for YOU.

The third step of recovering from abuse is perhaps one of the most difficult: giving up being "right" and being strong enough to admit when you're wrong. Let's face it—no one wants to be wrong, so much so that we fight just to be right. Countries wage wars and lives are lost all in the effort to be right. Giving up that need to be right freed my mind and allowed me to learn on a different level.

I had a certain righteous mindset, as do most victims have over their abuser. In my case, my father was wrong, and I was right. That was just the way it was. People were also wrong for judging me, and I had the right to be mad at them. And I held on to those beliefs for years.

I was not open to being wrong; my ego wouldn't allow it. I tried to forgive my father in my earlier years, but my ego got in the way. I couldn't forgive when I believed I was right. Forgiving Papa somehow meant that I was letting him off the hook.

I had to practice being okay with being wrong. Believe me; there was no shortage of opportunities. It seems that everything I did was wrong. One Friday, I picked up the kids for the weekend, grabbed a pizza for dinner, and headed home to watch their favorite TGIF lineup. The kids were sitting on the couch, eating, and watching television. I was eating at the dining room table and underwriting loans that I brought home for the weekend. About an hour into it, they were pleading with me to come and watch TV with them.

"I can't. I'm watching from here, and I have work to do," I replied.

A little while later, they asked again. "Mom, we never get to spend time with you."

"I'm right here. We're spending time together. Come on, I have to work," I said, slightly annoyed.

"You're always working," they grumbled.

I was ready to put my foot down with "keep it up, and you'll be going to bed early." But I paused for a moment, and I realized they were right. It's their time with me, and I should give them my undivided attention. But it was hard for me to admit that I was wrong. I wanted the coward's way out. *Just stop working and go over and spend time with them; they'll never know you were wrong. They're kids,* I thought.

That's when I had an ah-ha moment. Surprisingly, I had a problem with being wrong. Seemingly open-minded people can have a problem with admitting when they're wrong. I was no exception. Sure, they were kids and would never know that I was wrong, but I needed to be an adult and work on this. I knew I couldn't take the coward's way out.

Closing up my work for the night, I said, "Make room. I'm coming over." As I sat down, I said, "You guys are right. This is our time, not work time. I'm sorry. I was wrong for taking away your time with me."

"Mom, are you done? You don't have to work all weekend?" Laila asked.

"I don't have to this weekend," I smiled.

"Yeah! Omes! Omes! Mom doesn't have to work!" Laila shouted.

"Oh, mom, can we build a fort" Ome's chimed in as they danced around giddily. Smiling, I joined them, realizing *I'd rather be happy than be right.*

Although I was staying open to being wrong, it wasn't easy for me to admit. Then another ah-ha moment hit me. I had apologized a lot in my life. Saying "I'm sorry" had been part of my daily vocabulary for as long as I could remember.

"I'm sorry I'm late."

"I'm sorry I hurt your feelings."

"I'm sorry you didn't like that."

I had no problem apologizing. But I'd never said, "I was wrong." And I started wondering what it was about saying "I was wrong," that made my body sulk as if to melt away and made me ashamed to look the person in the eye. *Why did those words bother me?*

I know people make mistakes, and no one's perfect. So why did I still struggled to admit any wrongdoing out loud? After improving my self-awareness, I discovered that I had interpreted "I was wrong" as "I'm wrong, something is wrong with me. Therefore, I am bad." But why did I feel like I'm a terrible person? What was so wrong about me?

I definitely made terrible choices, and I did bad things. But doesn't everyone make mistakes? And isn't making mistakes part of the human experience? Don't all the monotheistic faiths (Judaism, Christianity, and Islam) as well as Eastern religions teach about repenting after you've done something wrong? So why did I still feel like a bad person?

Apparently, I had forgiven everyone in my life except myself. Parts of me were still holding on to self-hate. I declared that I was a work in progress, then I worked hard to enact that mindset.

One way I practiced being wrong and admitting to it was by reframing. Instead of saying, I'm right, or you're wrong, I said, "I'm going to forget everything I know, and let's see what I can learn." I had to fight with my ego, which was very powerful in fighting to survive and stay alive. Whenever I became combative and righteous, I immediately recognized it as my ego. The only thing that died when I admitted that I was wrong was my ego. This again freed me to go on the path of forgiveness.

The remaining steps are not actions. Instead, they are areas of exploration. Once I got cleared on an event/traumatic moment/what happened, I committed to changing my outlook. Throughout my journey of transformation, I continued exploring areas of concern. When I was having a difficult time with forgiveness, I reexamined and challenged my beliefs around it. Then I reframed it or created a more powerful meaning that worked for me.

I explored and stayed aware of how I felt when I had to forgive Papa or anyone else. To truly forgive, I had to know what I was forgiving; otherwise, I'd just be sweeping it under the rug. That's what I had done when I thought I had forgiven him years earlier. But it wasn't true forgiveness because I was still holding on to the righteous mindset. That's not forgiveness.

I first had to define what forgiveness is, compare that to what I thought it was, and reframe it to give it a new powerful meaning—one that either touched, moved or inspired me.

The meaning I had assigned to the word forgiveness was "to let someone off the hook." That is what I thought I had to do. Forgiving Papa meant saying it's okay, let bygones be bygones, and as much as I wanted that, I also wanted to hold him accountable. But I thought forgiveness would negate that.

I made a list of what it cost me to hold on to the pain, and the payoff or what I was getting out of holding on to the pain. Holding on was costing me my happiness, my ability to love myself, and my peace. The payoffs were that I got pity, and people felt sorry for me. But the biggest payoff was I got to blame Papa for my unhappiness, and I won the right to be right. That's it. For all my unhappiness, in the end, I got the honor of saying, "I'm right! It's your fault."

I reframed forgiveness to mean "letting myself off the hook." I no longer wanted to be affected by another person's behavior. And the way I saw it, I had to forgive him for not loving me the way I expected, for not protecting me in the way I expected. And I had to ask him for his forgiveness for thinking he was incapable of loving his own child. When I truly forgave, there were no vengeful thoughts. There was no holding on to the trump card. There was only empathy, compassion, love, and understanding.

I came to understand that forgiveness is also a journey, not one single moment in time. Depending on how much hurt, pain, and resentment I was holding on to determined how quickly I was willing to forgive or let it go. It took a while to work through forgiving my father and no time at all to forgive my friend, who had said some hurtful words to me in the heat of an argument. The forgiveness journey also isn't a straight road. Sometimes it is an uphill climb with some backsliding along the way.

Taking responsibility for my happiness instead of blaming others put me in the driver's seat of my life. I am responsible for how my life turns out. There is no more blaming anyone. I came to realize that blame is the coward's way out because there was no action. I was not an active participant in my happiness. Being responsible forced me into action—I had to make difficult choices and accept the consequences knowing that I had a choice. Even if the outcome may not be what I wanted, or it seemed like there was no choice, I still had a choice.

It was my choice to sneak out of the house to go to the library and study, even though the consequences were detrimental. It was my choice to get married, even though it felt like it wasn't. It was also my choice to leave my marriage, even if it meant leaving my children for a short time. None of those circumstances were ideal. But that's the point!

Like many of the people I've spoken to, we're often waiting for the right moment to make a move. One of my friends once said, "I'll leave when the children are older." And I said, "When I become rich, I'll travel the world." But there is no right time. There is no *someday* or *one day*. Those days do not exist. There is only today, and it's the right time when I (you) say it's the right time.

Living in the past is like driving while continually watching the rearview mirror. It's almost certain you will crash. Most of us think that we live in the present while planning for the future. But if we carry unresolved past trauma, we are really living in our past, thinking it's the present. Our future then becomes a reflection of the past. And it looks like more of the same or that nothing ever changes.

I couldn't be fully present during my marriage because my past haunted me without even knowing it. I brought the past into the present and put it directly in front of me as my future when I transferred my father's unresolved feelings onto my husband. Because I was dealing with my father's issues with my husband, the future with my husband looked like more of the same. Nothing changed.

Through my transformational journey, my connections with people during my travels, and my pastoral psychology studies, I have concluded that the unexamined ideologies passed down from generations are faulty. Ideals about love, compassion, trust, and religion have been misguided. I firmly believe that if we examine our core values, ideologies and reframe them to something that makes sense in our lives, we would change the conversation for the next generation.

I'd always been confused about love, compassion, and trust. The ideologies about these fundamental human values passed down from generation to generation did not make sense to me, or they had conflicting ideas. I had difficulty figuring out what love, compassion, and trust were because their definitions did not match the behavior and examples. For instance, love conquers all, have compassion for others, and only trust people that you know all sounded wonderful in theory, but challenging to maneuver in reality. I had to figure out what these fundamental values meant to me and how I would incorporate them into my life. These three core values, when practiced, comprise what I call my spiritual self or spirituality.

Defining Love, Compassion, and Trust

So, what is love? What is compassion? What is trust?

My work in transformation led me to reexamine these questions and make them understandable for myself. I encourage you to do the same.

Love is acceptance.

What is love? Do you first have to put love into categories before defining it, such as romantic love, family love, love of a child, etc.? The Bible states: "Love is patient and kind; love is not envious or boastful, or arrogant or rude. It does not insist on its own way; it is not irritable or resentful; it does not rejoice in wrongdoing, but rejoices in the truth ... Love never ends" (KJV 1 Cor. 13:4-8a).

Or is love what my grandmother said? "God is love, so that means Love is God"? We can all agree that showing love is a godly thing to do. But what about those who don't believe in God? Does that mean that they don't experience love?

My first experience of love happened when I was four. I can't tell you what I was thinking, but I still remember the way I felt. Hugs and kisses, laughter, and excitement—it was a joy that was so freeing. I was free to be, and people loved me just for me.

All the times in my life where I felt loved, I also felt accepted. I wanted children to have someone to love me, but my children have taught me how to love. I love them no matter what, and I would not change a thing about them. I accept them just as they are. I came to define love as acceptance. I accepted Papa just as he was, someone who wanted better for his family and had a bad temper. I accepted him with all his flaws, but it doesn't mean I accepted his behavior.

Love in all its form is basically energy. When we put out love, we are sending out positive energy. The energy is dispersed into the universe, snowballing into more and more positive energy. Changing the vibrations and creating harmony within the universe.

When someone says I loved you, but I'm not in love with you, it's a confusing statement. Because once we expel the energy, it's there forever. That love vibration has already been sent.

Compassion is action without judgment.

The Latin root for the word passion is *pati*, which means "to suffer." The prefix *com-* means "with." Thus, *compati* means to "to suffer with," "suffer together," or "co-suffering." Compassion or co-suffering goes beyond the understanding of another person's suffering. A compassionate person feels compelled to do something to help or relieve the suffering they are confronted with. This connection of suffering with another person brings compassion that moves beyond sympathy into the realm of empathy. Thus, compassion is a characteristic of love. If I'm compassionate, I'm also showing love.

When I feel compassion for those around me, it's difficult to stand by and watch them suffer. I'm motivated to help stop the pain, yet not every situation is solvable with my intervention. Sometimes the best way to help is to listen compassionately, but the listening must occur without judgment or expectation. I make eye contact letting the other person know that I see them. Then I listen, without any rebuttals, solutions, or judgments.

Practicing compassion every day has become part of my daily routine, like asking the checkout clerk at the grocery store how her day is going. And thanking her for her help in bagging my groceries—or offering water and food to the homeless guy who stopped me at the traffic light. These small acts connect me to others, and those acts let others know in the slightest way that I appreciate them. You cannot fake compassion because it's a natural and sincere part of love.

Trust is keeping your power.

Throughout my life, I had been taught not to trust anyone, and if I were going to trust someone, they would have to pass the litmus test for trust. The litmus test involves asking how long I know this person and what I know about them? The length of time and familiarity makes them a more trustworthy person.

It's easier to trust someone you've known for twenty years instead of someone you had just met one month ago. *But is that true? Can I trust a person whom I've known since childhood more than the person I just met?*

Many married men and women have cheated after twenty or thirty years of marriage. Many children who were molested had predators who were close to the family. And what about the religious community? Many priests have broken that sacred trust, resulting in molestation and rape being rampant throughout the Catholic Church. *So, if the length of time and familiarity can still produce mistrust, how am I supposed to know whom to trust?*

My answer came from raising my children. I've always taught them to do what's best for them. I imagine most parents tell their kids the same thing. But what happens when that child grows up and wants to move away for a good job? Should they pass up a great opportunity because it would hurt their mom if they lived so far away? Of course not. The child (now an adult) must do what is right for him. And his mom should support him.

The essence of that old ideology of trust is that when I say "I trust you," what I'm really saying is, "I give you my power called trust, and I know that you will do what's right for me even if it's not in your best interest."

That's an unspoken expectation. So when the person you have handed over your power to (like a partner in a relationship) acts in his/her best interest (which is what they've been taught to do), and it doesn't suit your needs, you get the privilege of saying "you broke my trust." After all, people will always do what's right for them. So, where does that leave us?

When our trust is broken, we feel a loss of power, and we end up blaming the other person without any resolution. We tend to make it all about them—He/she did this to me. This led me to look at trust as a loss of power. I have come to believe that trust has two components. The first part is to understand that everyone will do what is best for him/her; therefore, the second part of trust is that you must do what's right for you. You must trust yourself by knowing how to get out of the situation if it doesn't go your way.

At one point in my life, I dated this guy who was a friend of my friend; they'd known each other for many years. She had trusted him, so it was easy for me to trust him too. About three months into the relationship, one Friday night, we were hanging out at his place. I had never been there before. He left briefly to get something from his car. His house phone rang while he was downstairs, and I answered it. It was a girl who was asking for my boyfriend. I told her he'd be right back and asked if I could take a message. I wondered who she was, and she said she was his girlfriend. She explained that she was away and thought she would stay the weekend but decided to come back that Saturday night rather than Sunday. She wanted him to pick her up from the airport. I couldn't believe what I was hearing! *Does he have a girlfriend?*

I felt my heart racing faster and faster with each word she spoke. The heat of anger rose from behind my neck. I managed to tell her that I was his girlfriend, and we'd been dating for three months. They'd been together for almost a year. When he returned from his car, I was so hurt and angry that I couldn't hide it. I confronted him and kept asking "why," telling him he broke my trust as I cried and sobbed. I thought, *Why would he do this to me?* I felt powerless.

That experience was a pivotal moment in reframing trust. That experience taught me that I handed over my power to him when I said I trusted you.

What if dating two people were the best thing for him? He was doing what's best for himself; it had nothing to do with me. I probably was never even a thought. Why did I feel the need to say, "I can't believe you did this to me"? When, in reality, he did it to himself because he cheated himself out of having me.

Regaining my power, I was able to tell him, "You did what's best for you; it was your choice. Now that I have this information, I have to do what's best for me." This is my choice, and I broke up with him, powerfully. I kept my power. I never got an answer to why he did it, and I realized I never would. What possible explanation could he give me that would make me say, "Oh, okay, I see why you cheated"? I determined it was a useless question meant to keep us in agony.

Trusting in yourself when everything seems to be going wrong is the real test of adversity. It's only with trust that we can grow far beyond our limitations. It moved me from *I don't trust anyone* to *I trust that everyone will do what is right for them; therefore, I have to do what's right for me.*

I've grown to see trust, not as something we break or lose. I now see trust as the power to know yourself and to know you can take care of yourself.

After reframing these essential questions about love, compassion, and trust, that paralyzing dark hole that had sucked every ounce of joy from me and tormented me my entire life was instead filled with love, compassion, and trust. It lit me up. I was finally happy!

As my life began to change and take shape, my passion for traveling, and my dream of becoming a doctor were rekindled. I planned to finish my education, take care of myself and my children, and see the world.

I felt happy with myself, with the person I'd allowed myself to become. I was my own person with my own choices.

Not in my wildest dreams did I imagine life getting any better. But it did! Discovering the gift of travel and how it magically joined my two passions. Connecting with people and experiencing other cultures. Traveling allowed my soul to soar as I took chances and discovered a whole new world.

Chapter Ten

> "The world is a book and those who do not travel read only one page." —*St. Augustine of Hippo*

A Whole New World

My transformational learning made me ready to buy my first solo ticket to discover the world. *Where do I go first? There so many places to see!*

I made a list of the seven ancient wonders of the world and was adamant that I would visit them all, or at least what's left of them. I also wanted to learn as I traveled, adding some purpose to my adventures. I saw traveling as a beautiful way to connect with all that the world had to offer. I decided to learn about God and spirituality. I was interested in knowing what others thought about fundamental questions, like God and spirituality, and how they navigated their lives around that. Other perspectives were crucial to my continued growth.

Not being aware of the conflict but having read a lot on religions, I planned a trip that would cover the religious paths of Judaism, Christianity, and Islam. The words of my Naani stayed with me all those years. She'd cultivated a mindset of openness when it came to religion, and my reading had inspired me to see the world's wonders for myself. These factors culminated in a deep yearning to know God personally to form my unique relationship with Him.

For my first time leaving the country alone, I chose to travel to Egypt and Israel. Ecstatic and on top of the world, I was thrilled to have the freedom to live my life.

My fascination with Egypt awoke after seeing *The Ten Commandments* when I was younger. Of course, arriving at Cairo airport with a Trinidadian passport caused an uproar. The immigration officers weren't sure where Trinidad was, and a debate ensued over what African country it could be. After two hours, my tour guide came to inquire about me. He was fluent in English and Arabic, among many other languages. A quick chat with the officers and they started laughing and looking at me apologetically. One officer offered a handshake, and in less than ten minutes, I was out of the airport and walking toward our tour bus.

My tour guide told me with a smile that the immigration officers thought I was from a village in Africa, coming to work as a prostitute in Cairo. He explained it's a growing trend as poverty-stricken families need their girls to work. He also pointed out that it's rare to find a Muslim woman traveling alone, at least in this part of the world. We chuckled and instantly became friends. Returning to the United States, it was clear that being an American citizen would make traveling easier. (By the end of the next year, I became a proud U.S. citizen.)

My tour arrived at the Omar Khayyam Palace operated by Marriott. It was on the banks of the Nile, and it felt surreal. All of it—the history, sights to be seen, and a view overlooking the magical Nile with the silky city lights shimmering on the surface. I felt beautiful for the first time in my life, like Cleopatra herself.

My guide was kind and offered to show me a little magic outside of the tour. Giza was a close drive from the hotel, so he picked me up and took me to see the pyramids at night. He drove me to what looked like a partition fence and asked me to look through a decent-sized hole on one panel.

Wow! I sighed. "That's amazing!" I said, amazed.

The enormous Sphinx looked majestic, rising out of the ground and heading to the stars through the hole. Then came the tears of joy and astonishment and gratitude, all rolled into one. We finished the night with street food from vendors that lined the street along with the locals.

It was four in the morning, and two hours into my sleep, I was peacefully awakened by the sweetest sound—the call of the adhan, or the Muslim call to prayer. Jumping out of my bed, I headed for the terrace to listen more closely. I hadn't heard the adhan called in open air since my early childhood in Trinidad.

Immediately, I recognized the gift bestowed on me. There was a tug at my soul, pulling me toward my faith. Standing on my balcony, watching the men rush to one of the many nearby mosques. Maybe it was the Egyptian air, mixed with the smell of incense, and the natural beauty of the Nile, but there was a feeling of peace, exoticness, and mystery that somehow left me feeling immensely confident. I was unafraid because God was guiding me, and He felt so close to me.

The next morning, we headed out to explore Cairo. Nestled in the Sahara Desert, the majestic pyramids of Giza overtook the landscape. Climbing up about thirty steps, we could enter one of the pyramids. The experience made me feel like Indiana Jones entering the narrow, stifling entryway hidden in the rock. We crawled through small spaces to get to the chamber room, imagining all the treasures that once sat there in safety. After a trip inside the pyramid, I headed down the road for a camel ride across the shifting golden sand dunes. I did take a few moments to bask in the glory of the desert's vastness.

There were also the step pyramids of Saqqara; they were the first pyramids ever built and older than the pyramids of Giza. And finally, I came up close and personal with the majestic Sphinx, the broken-nosed half lion, half pharaoh crouching as a sentinel in front of the pyramids. I made sure to reserve my seat for the highly recommended laser show before wandering to the temple to find the perfect spot away from the crowds to soak in the views.

Climbing the great pyramids and walking in the footsteps of Moses and the pharaohs somehow made me feel like royalty yet spiritual at the same time. It was like time travel. And a trip to this holy land was fulfilling for my soul.

Later that week, we visited the Egyptian museum. King Tutankhamun's blue and gold mask was the highlight as it was one of the wonders retrieved from his tomb in the Valley of the Kings in 1922. The museum was crowded with artifacts from pharaohs before and after King Tut's rule.

On my free day in Cairo, my tour guide dropped me off at the famous Khan el-Khalili bazaar. I entered on foot through the historical Bab al-Futah gates, completed in 1087. Then I walked down a road lined with centuries-old mosques and crowded with tourists and locals. The merchants themselves were busy and colorful. It was my first experience haggling for scarves, alabaster sculptures, and Islamic clothes. Omie was intrigued by the magnificent mosques, so I started collecting beautiful Mosque drawings from every country with him. My exhausting battle with the merchants and the young hagglers bidding for my attention made me tired and hungry. I ended up at the El Fishawy Café, which I'd seen on the Travel Channel. Their freshly made falafel sandwich and ice-cold Coke quenched my thirst.

One cannot come to Egypt without taking a trip down the Nile, the world's longest river. One evening, I traveled via a felucca, or a traditional boat, down the Nile to Luxor. The banks, along the way, were lined with temples and merchants peddling their crafts. I jumped off the boat for a quick dip in the Nile: can now say I swam in the Nile. There's a saying in Egypt that if you drink from the Nile, you'll return. I had swallowed a fair amount of water while swimming in the river. And I fulfilled the prophecy twelve years later and then again when my daughter turned thirty.

Early the next morning, I'd arrived in Luxor, ready to start my day. Temples were the main attraction, but it was also the place to pick up authentic porcelain scarabs and alabaster statues. The first stop on the itinerary was Karnak Temple, a sprawling complex where you'll find obelisks, sacred lakes, sphinxes, and an incredible open-air hall of columns. The original traces of color were still visible. We rounded out the daylight by returning to watch the sunset on the temples. We're not allowed to take photos at the Valley of the Kings, and the guides were not allowed to go inside the tombs. So, I sat on a bench under a shaded tree and listened attentively as my guide explained the history of the Valley of the Kings.

Next was the tomb of Ramesses IX. I'm glad I had rested up before that. Seeing a king's tomb from thousands of years ago was mind-boggling. The hieroglyphs on the tombs were phenomenal. The colors looked like they were freshly painted, vibrant with personality and stories to be told. As I entered his tomb, I imagined Rameses from *The Ten Commandments* movie and how powerful he was. I wondered if he knew Moses. I perused the rest of the tomb in silence and awe.

Over eight nights, I'd traveled down from Cairo to Aswan and then to Luxor with six strangers on the cruise who had become lifelong friends. I caught the traveling bug and vowed to travel at every opportunity.

Judaism

The second half of my trip was to the Holy Land of Israel. When I was book-ing my trip to Egypt, it came with the option of a stop in Israel for only a few hundred dollars more. It was something I knew I couldn't pass up.

I never paid much attention to the political and religious conflict that surrounds Israel and Palestine. Our mosque and my Islamic community were not involved in that way. I never attended a rally or learned about the history of Israel. Ignorance is indeed bliss, and I'm glad I didn't know the story be-cause it allowed me the space to see the country, people, and religious culture without bias.

The Old City of Jerusalem was my first stop. There was so much to see. This square in Jerusalem's heart contains the Wailing Wall, the Dome of the Rock, and the nearby Church of the Holy Sepulchre. The air filled with Gregorian chants, the adhan calling the faithful to prayer, and the wailing from the nearby Wailing Wall.

The square had a unique fragrance—a mixture of musk oil, incense, and strong Arabic coffee brewing nearby. The maze of narrow streets, alleyways, and markets made up the heart of the city. The Old City is only one square kilometer and is surrounded by impressive Ottoman walls from the sixteenth century. Despite its size, it was easy to get lost.

Jerusalem's Old City is divided into four quarters: Jewish, Christian, Muslim, and Armenian. I experienced each district differently, appreciating each quarter's ambiance, culture, and history. It was all fascinating. I discov-ered some of the most significant religious sites in the world within those walls. And I completely allowed myself to get lost there, surrounded by the divinity.

I began exploring the Jewish Quarter, which is the most visited site for Jews. The Western Wall, known as the Wailing Wall, was built by Herod the Great over two thousand years ago. It sounded like a strange name, but the tour guide shared the story.

"Jews generally don't use the name Wailing Wall. It's known as the Western Wall or Ha Kotel, which is Yiddish for the wall. Some called it The Wall of Tears as it's a symbol of the Jewish temple's destruction. For centuries, Jews have come here to pray and cry in mourning."

I wanted to have the full experience by participating in all the rituals regardless of religion. I believe that there is only one God and that all religions pray to the same God even though they might call and worship Him differently.

I followed my Jewish friends from the tour to the relics of the Sacred Temple. Joining them as they followed the longtime practice of wedging small slips of paper between the wall's bricks. The paper contains your prayers and petitions for the wind to carry to the heavens.

The Jewish men were dressed in black, and their hair had long curly locks. They're called Hasidic Jews, and they form the most conservative branch of the religion. While praying, they rock back and forth. This symbolizes and mimics the candle's flame swaying and flickering as it attempts to tear free of its wick and ascend to heaven.

This divine swaying is common in other faiths as well. When I pray and call upon God in all His manifestations (the most merciful, most compassionate, etc.), my entire being becomes engulfed in peace, and my whole body sways automatically back and forth. Sometimes even with tears rolling down my cheeks as I become consumed in devotion. Sincere praying and devotion are a way for the body and mind to tune in with the soul to contact the divine.

I curiously observed everyone around me praying or meditating. Looking at the wall, I noticed the different styles of stonework. It was as if each stone wanted to tell me a story. I stood there, looking around in astonishment and wonder. There was a divine presence that was powerful, sincere, and peaceful, even if you are not a spiritual person.

Christianity

We headed beyond the Wailing Wall on the route to the Via Dolorosa, or the Way of Sorrows. I walked the path that Christ walked to Calvary. Entering from the Damascus Gate, I made my way to Lions' Gate where the Way of Sorrows began. The Old City can be confusing to navigate with the endless tourists and the residents going about their daily lives. Residents and tourists bumped into each other along the cobblestone lanes as they wandered through the *souk* (market).

The street market sprawled across Jesus's path. Centuries of interreligious bargains have been struck there. Merchants sell everything with a religious twist, even souvenir ashtrays bearing images of the faith of choice. There were also velvet paintings of the Last Supper, scrolls made of gold thread with Quranic verses, mother-of-pearl rosaries, and mother-of-pearl inlaid on carved olive wood and cedar camels. There were priestly sandals, Islamic prayer rugs, and what seemed out of place were various Aladdin-like brass oil lamps.

As soon as I entered the path through Lions' Gate with my guide, he pointed out St. Anne's Church on the right, built over the grotto where the Virgin Mary was born. Although it's not a Station of the Cross, it was a pleasant surprise. The Pools of Bethesda were next to the church. This place somehow felt more familiar than the mosque.

The acoustics of the church were incredible. Even whispers seemed to echo for several minutes. Our small group included four couples, a mother-daughter team, and me, the only single person in the group. Many visitors, including myself, held dual identities of tourists and worshipers. These religious sites were significant as I'd noticed we were all on our own spiritual journey, which required some solitude. Walking with my Jewish tour guide, the atmosphere was solemn with little chit chat, and lots of people held back tears while others openly wept. I did not hold back my feelings; I was so moved by everything that I cried at all the sites.

Each Station of the Cross is marked along the Via Dolorosa with Roman numerals. Numbers I through XIV encircle the sidewalks of every Catholic and Orthodox Church. The first eight stations are along the path from Lions' Gate and lead to the Holy Sepulchre Church. Stations nine through fourteen are on the grounds of the church. My tour guide pointed out that the city was built a city upon the city for centuries. The original street level where Christ would have walked is about twenty feet below the modern-day street level. But pilgrims didn't care about those details. They'd come to strengthen their faith, not question it.

Some Stations were off the street in surprising niches. We were led into the yard of a Muslim elementary school. That was the First Station of the Cross, where Jesus was condemned by the crowd that released Barabbas. A concave cobblestone in the center of a basketball court marked the sacred spot. The stone had worn smooth. I saw shoppers and kids on bikes at the edges of the yard and scattered newspapers with photos of war scenes. A few tourists knelt and touched a tiny grid gouged in the fieldstone.

The Second Station was across from the first, in the Franciscan Monastery. Two chapels mark the condemnation and flagellation of Christ. On Fridays, the Franciscan monks lead a procession down the Via Dolorosa starting from there as a reenactment.

A tractor towing a wagon of rolled-up rugs roared as it passed us. Someone had stacked egg crates and garbage sacks in the street, right below the Third Station plaque, where Jesus had fallen for the first time. A man carrying dozens of bread loaves in a clear plastic sack walked by with his shoes clicking briskly. A street vendor whispered, "Please, sir-r-r," insistently shoving religious booklets at passersby. The proprietor of a souvenir-and-food stall shouted from across the alley. "New Testament! Three dollars!"

Before the Armenian Church, twenty yards farther on, we came to the Fourth Station. That's where Jesus had met his mother, Mary. Directly across from it, before another shop, T-shirts swung like flags in the morning. One read: My Grandmother Went to Israel and All I Got Was This Lousy T-shirt.

Under a canopy, the Arab proprietor sipped tea. He's almost lost between high stacks of sheepskin booties, Bedouin headdresses, and more smart-ass shirts. Over a picture of an intact Solomon's Temple, one shirt said: Don't Worry—Israel will rebuild. A couple of steps away, we were told to put our hand into a palm-sized nook in a stone wall. That was Station Five.

"Here's where Simon of Cyrene helps carry the cross," our tour guide explained. The portable radio in the film-and-guidebook shop across the way was playing heavy metal music, spoiling the ambiance. Next door, at the olive wood workshop, woodworkers lathed "artifacts."

The Via Dolorosa turned off a street called El Wad, amidst more shops. Beyond the spot was a fruit stall where women were picking through stacks of oranges and almonds. More delicious scents swirled through the air, and there was more foodie eye candy in the piles of gleaming carrots and cabbages the size of a goat's head.

I imagined myself living in Jerusalem. It felt divine to walk the footsteps of the prophets. Families were living all around there, sometimes two or three families living together.

I walked past Station Six, where St. Veronica had wiped Jesus's face. It's marked by windows full of graphic statuary of the suffering Jesus.

Jesus had fallen for the second time at Station Seven. I stopped to take a picture of myself at the station. I had to be cautious not to get the lamb carcasses on me, from the awkwardly close butcher's stall next door. Peering out the window of a merchant's shop was a teenager with her veil drawn back, showing off her wistful smile and beautiful kohl-enhanced eyes.

We passed piles of purses, stacked copper pots, schools of salted fish, and refrigerator magnets. Coming out at the far end of the arch, we entered a crowded street market. I trotted a little to catch up with the group who was waiting for me at Station Eight. The guide teased, "This is where Jesus meets a group of women." I wondered how long he'd waited to say that. I rolled my eyes and smiled as we mounted the ramp-like stairs by a large sign that read ZALATIMO SWEETS.

Weaving in and out between children shooting marbles on the rough stone, I climbed up the rear porch of a youth hostel near Station Nine, where Jesus had fallen for the third time. We shook our heads at the European teenagers lounging shirtless on the hostel's rear deck. One older tour member muttered in distaste, "They drink beers there now."

Approaching the crème de la crème of Christianity, a half-dozen Christian sects were attending their faithful tasks. Their dominions were stacked and interwoven directly above the sacred ground of Calvary. An Ethiopian Orthodox Monastery lay atop the Holy Sepulchre Church. The nub of the great church dome snuck into the courtyard and a small cupola in the monastery yard. Far below was the Coptic, Greek, Armenian, and Roman sects sharing the cubic space of Holy Proximity for centuries.

The chapels were decorated with paintings of Solomon and Sheba. We entered the Coptic sanctuary below, then curled down more stairs into the grand Church of Holy Sepulchre. The last five Stations of the Cross were within this marbled maze.

At Station Ten, Roman soldiers had taken Jesus's robe. Roman Catholic territory started there and included the Eleventh Station, where a few feet away, Christ was nailed to the cross.

Farther along was the Greek Orthodox section. They controlled Station Twelve, where the cross had stood, and Station Thirteen, where Christ had been taken down.

The dimly lit church branched into side chambers. A priest was walking around with brass vases carrying incense everywhere. Fragrant, acrid pine incense wafted through all territories. All over the dusky walls was an overwhelming mishmash of sorrowful icons. Rose, tan, black, and white marble panels sat above scrolled railings.

"Do you want to touch the *real* Calvary, where it *really* happened?" my guide whispered to me. I smiled and nodded. He lifted the velvet skirt draped over a table of glimmering votive candles, lanterns, and statues. In the dimness below, I successfully navigated one hand. My fingertips slid into a slit the width of my palm then into a hole opening on the marbled floor. I squeezed my fingers down into it and felt the rough, cold stone of blessedness, warmed by candlelight. I glanced at the cold, sacred rock. A tourist stopped to speak with our tour guide, "Is this where the REAL THING happened?"

"Yes. Yes," the guide answered, unbothered by the unpaid tour. The woman's eyes opened wide. She was glowing like she'd hit the jackpot.

There was a nun on duty, her eyes glued and focused as she lovingly scraped the wax off thousands of candles recently bought, placed, lit, and spent. A thousand pleas for merciful intervention. By her side, an Orthodox priest in a black flowing robe offered more virgin candles to passersby. In our group, the teenager in pink pedal-pushers and red sneakers whispered while she giggled and pointed at the word virgin on the sign. She walked arm in arm with her mom as they spoke in wonder. "Is that where they washed Jesus's body?"

Unsolicited, I replied, "Yes, that's the rock."

"That's the *actual* rock?" the teenager asked in wonderment.

We were led to the tomb, the Fourteenth Station. There was a tiny hut, an ornate two-chambered mausoleum, free-standing, far beneath the huge church dome. In the tiny anteroom of the place rested the rock slab that had sealed, and then it came away from the tomb where Jesus had been placed. It was covered with a shield of thick plate-glass.

The older American Midwestern couple in our group touched the glass with their fingertips. They traced Jesus's body and then clenched each other's hands. A dark-robed Orthodox priest bent slowly down as though savoring a beckoning lover as he kissed the glass. He hovered over it for a whole two minutes, holding up the line. The line crowding up behind, no one dared disturb his quaint ecstasy. Two nuns placed their rosaries beside the priest's cheeks to capture proximate holiness.

I crouched as I entered the inner chamber of the hut—the tomb itself. A deep-eyed, somber, priest in a cassock attended the tiny room. He recognized our tour guide. He must see him about three or four times a day in the busy season.

"This is where Christ the Lord was buried," our guide explained.

"May I light a candle?" I asked.

"Yes, sure if you want," he replied. I lit a candle and prayed, then crouched and backed out discreetly.

Outside of the Church, the streets were bright and bustling. Boys were singing or chanting songs in Yiddish as the Arabic call to pray echoed in the air, calling the faithful to pray from the minarets of the Dome of the Rock Mosque.

Islam

Our guide took the short route to the Dome of the Rock. There was always a short route, weaving in and out of narrow cobblestone alleys to avoid the crowds. We eventually arrived at the Al-Aqsa Mosque. In front of the mosque was a row of pipes with a concrete sitting bench. Worshipers used the washing station to perform Wudu, the purification ritual required before the ritual prayer.

The Al-Aqsa Mosque sat outside the grand courtyard. It's also known as the Farthest Mosque. One night the angel Gabriel came to Muhammad while he slept near the Kaaba in Mecca. Gabriel presented him with the Buraq, which took him on a spiritual midnight journey called Hijrah.

That picture from our Trinidadian home that I'd wondered about decades earlier now made sense to me. Ironically, the Buraq looks a lot like the centaur. The astrological sign of Sagittarius, my birth sign. This winged horse landed on the spot now known as the Farthest Mosque, as that's the furthest the Buraq could go. Muhammad then climbed on the Rock. From that Rock, Muhammad journeyed to the heavens, where he met other prophets, such as Moses and Christ. He saw paradise and hell, and finally saw God enthroned and encircled by the angels. After he spoke to God, Muhammad then journeyed back by night.

The Dome of the Rock is one of the most controversial landmarks in Jerusalem. In a simple explanation, the Jews hold the site sacred because it's the site of Solomon's Temple. The Romans destroyed the temple. During the Muslim rule, the Muslims used the site to erect the Dome of the Rock on top of Solomon's Temple's remainder to symbolize Islamic dominance.

We arrived at the courtyard of the Dome of the Rock. It was simply magnificent! I took my time to absorb the atmosphere and wandered through the lovely gardens. At the dome, families gathered to pray or chat while their kids ran around. I was amazed by the interaction of people from different religions, and I was unable to tell who was Muslim, Jewish, or Christian until they greeted me. The Muslims greeted me with salaam, the Jews with shalom, and the Christians with a good morning. Women from all faiths were covered head to toe out of respect for the holy site.

Walking into the mosque, we passed mosaic tiles adorning every wall with motifs of flowers, vegetables, and winged crowns. In the center of the mosque was the large Rock, rising toward the dome. A short-gated barrier surrounds the Rock, making it easy to walk around. There's a spot open to tourists where you can touch a tiny part of the Rock.

Patiently I awaited my turn to caress the divine Rock. When I rubbed my hands gently on the smooth surface, it was as though I was soothing away my sins. I was told to sniff my hands afterward. My hands smelled as if I had dipped them in the most fragrant garden. I cannot describe the fragrance as I've never smelled anything so peaceful before or after. I concluded that must be what the divinity smells like.

The inscriptions adorning the top of the walls included Quranic verses with the word Bismillah (in the name of God) starting every verse. Some of the inscriptions also referred to Mary and Christ and proclaimed that Christ was a favored prophet. Thus, the inscriptions claimed some of the core values, at the time, was the newly formed religion of Islam.

Under the Rock was a small chamber with a purpose not yet fully understood. One theory is that it was the cave Prophet Muhammad sought refuge. Another belief is that it's where the Prophet Abraham rested while tending to his flocks. Either way, I was blessed enough to go in and pray. After the lines lessened, I was wandering around the cave entrance and trying to peek in. The rope barring the access didn't allow a good view. An old Arab man was dressed in the traditional thobe (a special garment), counting his beads like a rosary. He guarded the entrance. I smiled and bid him As-salaam Alaikum (peace be with you). He smiled back and replied with wa-Alaikum salaam (peace be with you too).

Looking around, he gestured, asking if I wanted to go in. In shock, I pointed inside, asking if I could go in. He quickly opened the rope and said, "Salaat, salaat." I took it to mean prayer only, so I rushed into the cave. Once inside, I was in a daze and couldn't believe that I was inside the holy cave, one where the prophets sought refuge. Catching my breath and sobbing the whole time while I performed my prayer, it felt so divine and sacred. I fell into a kind of gratitude—the kind where you feel undeserving of God's mercy. I questioned what I'd done to deserve such a gift, the incredible blessing to be in such a holy place. A place that transcended religion. A place where we were all divinely one.

Walking away from the space with endless gratitude and peace, I wondered if that could be a sign that God had forgiven me. *Could it be that I'm being rewarded after my suffering? Or maybe it was an invitation to know God and an opportunity to form my personal relationship with him.*

Our group departed to stroll toward the restaurant for dinner. Walking with my guide, I sensed that he wanted to ask me something but felt hesitant. Finally, he asked, "How are you religious?"

It did not make sense, but then I realized he was fumbling his words. He murmured something as we scrambled around an outdoor dining table reserved for us.

After some brief comments from the group about the places we visited, he got the courage to ask me, "Jamila, are you Muslim?" He was confused as I'd put a message at the Wailing Wall, lit a candle in the church, and even participated in washing someone's feet. He seemed puzzled as if to say you're not a real Muslim. "I'm a Muslim," I replied. The people in the group looked at me oddly. "Really," replied one group member. I sensed and understood why they would feel this way. Then, I told them about my grandmother, Naani, and what she had taught me about acceptance. But most importantly, what she instilled in me: "A true believer cannot be influenced away from his faith as long he believes that 'God is One and God is love.'"

The next day was the last day of the trip. I opted out of visiting the Jewish site, the Masada, to stroll and explore the city independently. It was quite different from what I had imagined. I stopped to watch a group of teenagers get belly button piercings. When I became hungry, I waltzed into a deli-style shop for a falafel sandwich. The man behind the counter looked at me and continued about his business. I asked for a sandwich, and he ignored me. Other people were coming in ordering in English with no problem. After about the fourth time I asked, he finally replied: "We don't serve Muslims here." Then he shooed me away.

Confused, I continued along my way to the shop opposite the deli. It was an old shop that sold jewelry and other Jewish religious items. The storekeeper struck up a conversation with me as I contemplated buying a menorah for my sister Liz. She married a Jewish man, and I thought this would be a lovely keepsake. After telling the storekeeper what had transpired at the deli, he shook his head in sadness and said, "We are not all like that." I sensed the discomfort in him like he somehow wanted to remedy the situation. Then, he handed me a pair of sterling silver earrings with a green teardrop stone. "This is the stone of Elaat, and it's my gift to you," placing it in my palms. "We are not all like that," he said again in the most apologetic way. He then informed me that the necklace I was wearing, which I purchased in Egypt, had my name written in Arabic, and it cued the deli man.

This magical trip to Egypt and Israel was the first of many trips over the years. So far, my transformation from the darkness of self-hate to self-love, I'd reframed old disempowering stories and ideologies and found new meaning for love, compassion, and trust. I'd explored areas around forgiveness and righteousness. My trip to Egypt and Israel offered insights into religion and God, but it also left me yearning for more. I didn't have a logical explanation of how I saw God or who He was for me. And I still wondered about the purpose of life and life after death. I knew this was a calling to strengthen my spiritual self.

Chapter Eleven

"We are spiritual beings having a human experience."
—*Pierre Teilhard de Chardin.*

The Spiritual Journey of the Soul

On my quest to strengthen my relationship with the Divine, I thought about leaving my religion and converting to Christianity. Maybe Christianity would be the answer. I recalled conversations I'd had with the nuns at my high school and with my other Christian friends, and their approach seemed very loving, which was very attractive to me. But, I decided to learn about Islam, and if it didn't make sense for me, then I'll revisit the idea of converting.

I was looking for a "softer" side of Islam, which I knew existed because the Prophet Muhammad (peace be with him) was said to be extremely loving and kind. He spoke softly and had an understanding of people's suffering in the world. I'd heard of Sufism, a mystical sect of Islam. Sufism focuses on the believer's personal experience with God and aims to create a union with God.

This curiosity took me to Konya, Turkey, the birthplace of Rumi. Rumi was the son of a renowned Sufi scholar, who taught his son about the Sufi way very early on. Sufism is primarily concerned with developing the spiritual or,

more precisely, the inner character. Both Rumi and his father were firm be-
lievers in the revelations of the Quran but criticized the mere outwardly legal
and ritual practices promoted at the time.

Much of Rumi's work was dedicated to waking people up, encouraging
them to experience life themselves, forming a personal relationship with their
Creator rather than blindly following the scholars of the day. One who is educated in Sufism and had dedicated his/her life to Sufism is called a Moulana
or master. My studies of Sufism led me to a Moulana in Turkey.

In Konya, the Moulana I studied with came out dressed in a white robe
with a white headdress resembling a turban. Smiling, he greeted me with his
right hand over his heart, bowing his head slightly. "As-salaam Alaikum," he
said as he looked straight into my eyes.

I was taken back. *Muslim men don't look you in the eyes,* I thought. He had
a good, welcoming aura about him that reminded me more of the Buddha.
We sat on the floor of an open gallery in the courtyard of the mosque.
Comfortable cushions and pillows adorned the area, making it an inviting,
reverent environment.

"Would you like some tea?" he asked as I sat down.

"No, thanks," I replied.

He sat opposite and facing me he smiled, and said in perfect English,
"What would you like to know?"

I didn't know where to start. "What is Sufism? I don't know much about
it, but I would like to know more."

"You must join our classes," he said.

"Classes?" I replied.

"Yes, Sufi is quite simple. But you cannot learn it in a couple of days. You
practice being a Sufi every day," he said.

I decided to join the classes which ran for seven days. Inside the one week
was a three-day retreat.

The Moulana's pleasant face and contagious smile made me feel relaxed
and open to asking him anything. On the day we met, I had burning questions
for him. So, I asked him about the differences between Sunni, Shiite, and Sufi
Muslims (the three sects of Islam)

The Moulana answered, "It's like this. Three people were walking to the
mosque, a Sunni, a Shiite, and a Sufi. They encountered an accident on their
way to prayer. The Shiite said, 'I'll call the ambulance, I can't be late for prayer.'
The Sunni said, 'I will wait here until the ambulance comes. It's okay if I'm

late for prayer.' Then the Sufi said, 'You guys go ahead, and I'll stay here as long as they need me. This is my prayer."

My arm filled up with goosebumps. I was so moved and inspired by his words.

"Wow," I said.

"If you can understand the meaning of what I just said, then it means you will understand the Sufi way. It's a practice that you practice in everything you do," he said.

I joined the three-day retreat with the Moulana as my teacher, and I learned many ways of looking at religion. We chatted extensively during the retreat, but we also spent a great deal of time silently walking in the gardens, observing nature. The retreat removed every fear I'd ever had about Papa. Any doubts I had about whether I made the right decisions regarding my divorce and children were all eliminated—ideas about not liking myself all melted away in that week, especially those three days. I knew my life would be different because something monumental had shifted in me. Until that point, religion had taught me that I should be afraid of God. But the retreat took my spirit to a new level. I formed a deeply personal and unique relationship with my Creator with my God. It made me feel special, and I went around saying: "God is my friend; we have a special relationship."

One of the most influential parts of the retreat was the Moulana's lessons about the soul and its journey. It was captivating. *Eureka! I've found it; I'd found my whole reason for being, for being born, for being on earth, and even where I'd end up.* The story of the soul's journey made perfect sense to me.

By the end of those seven days, I'd come to my own interpretations and understandings to solidify my faith. My knowledge of how and why I was created was finally crystal clear. I decided to live my life as a pure soul navigating the physical world.

During the week, I had gained a clear understanding of my purpose on earth. Why I was created, why I'm here on earth, and what it all means. This understanding of my soul helped me to center myself when life's hurdles get in the way. In a summary version, the journey sounds like this.

When Adam was created, God blew into his backbone, the seed of every soul that was to be born. That means every soul that has ever lived is living and has yet to live.

It's explained that the soul would travel through six lives and experience death only once. The first two lives are pre-birth, and the third life is our life on earth. How we live our earthly life will determine where we end up in the next three lives.

When all the souls were created at the time of Adam, the souls were sent off to live their first life. We are pure souls, like little bright lights bouncing around, unaware of any human conditions in the first life. There is no space and time. Or concepts of good or bad, or choices to disobey our Creator. In this world (the first world, that's where you and I dwell until it was our time), all the souls knew was to serve the Lord. We loved our Creator unconditionally, and the Creator loved us in return. Our souls basked in pure love, which made us happy, so we laughed a lot to shine our light everywhere.

The first world is indescribable and incomprehensible to humans. Some say it's like heaven or Jannah, or the Garden of Eden. We loved this world so much that we didn't want to leave. The angels spoke to us about the journey we would take during the six-life phase. You will experience life and death only once. And, we were promised that we would return to be with God according to how we lived our third life. There is an emphasis on the third world because how we live our life on earth will determine where we go after we die.

The third world is the earth. You will be trapped within a body and given a series of tests. If you live and act from love, you will pass the test, the angels said.

The Lord explained, "Because when you love me, you will remember me and worship me. And you will come to talk to me often. But if you forget me, then you will fall into the trapping of the Human body and its needs."

The angels continued explaining this to the pure souls, "God will give you everything you need to pass the test. You will be given parents (two people) who will help you until you can do it on your own, and everyone you meet along the way will be your test as you will be a test for them. And as mercy, God created for you an acclimation period. This will be your second life."

The angels explain to the pure souls that they will leave the first world and enter the second world through their mother's womb. "This is where you get acclimated with the body. Your body will grow around your soul. You will begin to feel human emotions, but your mother will take care of all your needs. You will start to hear your mother's voice, and that will comfort you. Your mother has a special place as heaven lies at the feet of your mother. You will begin to love this second world so much, and you will not want to leave as you didn't want to leave the first world. You will have one birth into your life on earth, which is our third world."

Have you ever seen babies smile and laugh for no reason? They are living from their souls. They show you unconditional love, and they are so excited when they discover a new body part. They are like little balls of bouncing light playing with their tiny body, happy to discover new things, and laugh and entertain themselves.

This is indeed God's mercy to be born into a small body and grow into the body that you need to complete your test. It would be a scary thing to skip the second life and be born an adult. How would our tiny souls feel when they see a fully formed body with its massive ribcage as bars to entrap their souls? Indeed, God's plan is perfect.

Finally, it made sense when people say, "all you need is love." That phrase used to confuse me, but now it's taken on real meaning. If we live with the same love we were created from in our present third world, we will be home scot-free for the remaining three lives.

Another one of God's mercies to humans is that He promised to guide us to remember Him. Different religions and philosophies have their ways of prayer and worship. But some believe that God does not exist. And those who don't associate their beliefs to any religious tradition. Yet, they can still be kind, compassionate, and loving human beings. They exemplify love by taking care of their environment, their neighbors, and themselves. They volunteer and give back to their communities, and they condemn crimes against humanity. Whether they believe it or not, they are serving and honoring God. The Sufi teaches that kindness is an act of love; thus, it is worship.

The remaining three lives are also indescribable, so humans cannot comprehend them. Like our inability to understand where we came from.

Humans will experience death only once in these six lives. The angels warned us that we would come to love this world so much that we will not want to leave. Just as we loved the worlds before and did not want to leave. As humans, we get attached to things and people that we love. We don't want to live without them. When someone dies at a young age, we say, "gone too soon," and we mourn the death a bit differently than one who passes at an old age. With the former, there's a feeling of unfairness, leaving us to ask why. But we must understand that no time is too short, that every living creature, every soul will return to its Creator when the time is right. We must know that God's timing is not our timing, and we must believe that one's life, whether long or short, was part of our test. Then we can look for lessons that will deepen our understanding of ourselves and our purpose.

When we die, the soul is released from the body and goes into the fourth world as souls. Unlike the first world, the fourth world's soul has all the memory and knowledge that it had on earth. But they don't have an ego; therefore, they don't have emotions like hatred, anger, and pain. For many years, I feared seeing my father when I died. I was afraid of who he was in the human world. But now, knowing that he was a soul capable of only love, I'm comforted that I will see him again.

In the fourth world, we are reunited with the souls that have passed on; the angels continued. You will meet with your loved ones and catch up while waiting for your other loved ones to come. Your grandmother may ask, "how is my grandchild?" Or she may ask about other family members. At this point, the soul misses the people they've left behind, and they can appear to them in dreams.

There is a dream world hovering between the heavens and earth. This dream world is where Prophet Muhammad (peace be with him) is said to have received his revelations of the Quran. It's where divine messages were sent to Prophet Joseph, which he interpreted. A soul can provide guidance after obtaining the permission of the angels. Again, there is no concept of space and time in the fourth world, and they once again can move freely. This world is a waiting place until the trumpet is blown. The angels will then tell the souls when the time has come to reunite with their bodies. That will be the fifth world.

Once reunited in the fifth world, the trumpet will sound. All the souls, including humans, animals, and every living creature, will come together. Here in the fifth world, you will not be concerned with anyone. You will not want to see your parents or children or loved ones because you will not help anyone. You're only worried about facing God and answering for your actions on earth. It's described that you will not be able to see God. There will be a veil between God and the judging soul. It's said that during your judgment, the angels, prophets, and loved ones will testify for or against you.

Our body will also testify by saying what it did. If you stole on earth, your hands would testify that they were commanded to take that which does not belong to him. If you lie, your tongue will testify that you made it spread false rumors.

It's recommended that when you travel, you should pray in the land you touch. Because the earth will stand up for you and say that you prayed on that soil, similarly, if you destroy the earth, they will testify that you littered or spat on them.

At the end of your judgment, you will see your deeds on earth and how you handled them. And there will be no doubt which life you deserve. According to your deeds, you will end up in heaven or Jannah in a form that you cannot imagine, and your soul will live on forever. Again, you will be able to see God and live with Him. That is the sixth world.

If you end up in hell, you will remain there until there are enough souls to testify for your release. This is the reason we are urged to pray and forgive those who have passed on. And for Muslims, it became a duty to educate their children in Islam because your children will pray for you after your death.

The Traveling Soul

By the turn of the century, my new life had brought me independence, self-confidence, and travel. I had traveled to forty countries around the world.

My trip to India was very emotional. I thought about Papa at every turn. It was his dream to visit India and see where he came from. I thought about the book I'd read about the colorful people of Rajasthan my whole time there.

I'd sat on the cold marble and marveled at the undying love marked by the Taj Mahal. I'd rode an elephant and came in close contact with a Bengal tiger on an Indian safari. From a boat, I watched the sun sparkle as it rose over the calm Ganges River.

I'd climbed three hundred steps to have dinner with the monks in Nepal. And I glimpsed at the majestic Himalayan mountains from my room.

I'd fed the pigeons in Trafalgar Square, watched the changing of the guards at Buckingham Palace, and strolled under London Bridge.

I'd eaten fresh seafood in Lisbon, paella in Spain, and couscous in Morocco. I got my hands hennaed by Marrakesh's gypsies, and I'd performed in a mock traditional Moroccan wedding in Fez.

I had coffee in a café in Gibraltar and ate dinner on top of the Eiffel Tower and indulged in gelato in Rome. I'd tossed a coin in Trevi Fountain. Ate the best pasta in the world and shopped in fashionable Milan.

I'd walked on the Great Wall of China. Practiced tai chi at the Shaolin Temple and burned incense at Purple Heaven Palace in Wudang's mountains.

I'd snorkeled in the Red Sea, the Caribbean, and the man-made caves of Xcaret. I'd cruised the Mediterranean through the Greek Isles and basked in the sun in Cypress. I'd strolled through the ancient ruins of Greek civilizations, visiting the gods of their time.

I'd danced to my heart's content at the original Copacabana in Cuba, the Hard Rock café in London, and the night-clubs in New York.

All those trips made me believe in myself more. And in every place I visited, I'd always made time to sit and talk with the locals. I've met many remarkable people in my global travels. And I've had in-depth conversations with many women about their lives, their joys, and their sorrows. Recurring themes emerged everywhere, whether in rural India or fashionable Milan: hopelessness, insecurities, and loss of power.

While driving through Rajasthan to Jaipur's Pink City, our tour bus had to stop to change a tire. As the group sat on the side of the road, I watched a young girl followed by two little toddlers as she made her way from the lake, carrying water on her head. She piqued my interest. They were as curious about us as we were of them.

Slowly we made friends with the young girl and asked her to come to sit with us. She promised she'd be back. After ten minutes or so, she showed up with six teenagers. In my group, the two ladies decided to wait it out on the bus where there was air conditioning. I sat with the young girls, their eyes bright, illuminated by their infectious smiles. I asked them to tell me about their lives. Between their broken English and my bad Hindi, we were able to communicate. The young girl I first saw carrying the water was only thirteen, and the two toddlers were her kids. She lived with three of the girls who came with her. She told me that there is a house in the neighborhood made for girls like her to live in.

"What do you mean, girls like you?" I asked, thinking she was perhaps an orphan living in an orphanage.

"For girls who are unwed and have children, like us," as she pointed to her friends.

It was incomprehensible. As she told me, she was around ten and a half when one of the men in the village raped her, and she became pregnant. Her father threw her out of the house and cut ties with her for disgracing them. After she had the baby, she was newly freed prey and got attacked again. She was forced to bring yet another child into the world. The other six girls were in similar situations, so they'd gathered and built a mud hut no bigger than a kitchen.

My heart was broken, but I commented on how I admired them for banding together to make a house to live in because that was better than living in the streets. We talked for about an hour. They told me that something was wrong with them because there are girls who never got molested. We continued chatting, and one by one, they broke down.

"Aunty, you don't understand. My destiny is already set. There's nothing I can do about it. There is no choice."

"We know we can never be happy, so we don't think about it."

Another girl said, "Right now, I'm happy. I'm very happy to meet you."

Smiling, I asked why.

She replied, "Because no one ever stops to talk to us. We are untouchables, the lowest of the caste system."

"It's true, Aunty," another girl chimed it. By now, my heart was shattered. I could only imagine what their self-talk was saying to them.

As I was called to get on the bus, I told them, "You are worthy of love and kindness. You're God's child, so feel proud of yourself. I love you." And I hugged each of them, which made them sob. I left them with a little token of my appreciation. I could see the sadness in their faces as we drove away. My heart felt so broken and so sad it bothered me on all levels.

Stories of deprivation from food, education, and even love were common themes throughout my travels. All those things had left women powerless in their lives. And that was not good enough for me.

I shared my experiences and listened to women from around the world. Regardless of their different religions and cultures, they had remarkably similar stories of hopelessness, insecurities, and loss of power.

That led me to my passion: helping women reclaim their power and live a life they love. Immediately after graduating with my master's degree in Counseling Psychology, I enrolled in a doctoral program to become a Pastoral Psychologist. Combining psychology and religion was the perfect fit. I honestly believe it has been the most beneficial for my clients. As humans, we are mind, body, and soul, and I would treat the mind and soul with psychological modalities religion and or spirituality.

Pursuing my passions and purpose helped me feel whole again, even more successful than I imagined I could be. And that opened my heart to a new love.

Chapter Twelve

"Love recognizes no barriers. It jumps hurdles, leaps fences, penetrates walls to arrive at its destination full of hope." —*Maya Angelou*

Love at Last

"Come rest in my store," he said in the calmness tone. His words were like whispers echoing through the alleys, softly landing on my heart.

I stopped in my tracks, frozen for a moment in time. Something was pulling me towards him even though I hadn't seen his face.

"Keep talking," I replied, turning over my left shoulder, waiting to hear his soothing and inviting voice. I was basking in the overwhelming fullness within my heart. I was so mesmerized by his voice that the desire to actually see his face at that moment was not imperative.

"Come, have a cup of tea in my store. I won't try to sell you anything," he continued. My heart told me to trust him. *How can a stranger's voice all of a sudden feel like a missing part of me?*

"If I turn around and you're good looking, I'm going to marry you," I said boldly. Turning around, I saw that he wore the most dashing, ear-to-ear smile.

Thank God, he's handsome. My inner voice was elated. He was the sexiest man I'd ever met. Medium build, a cleft chin, and dreamy eyes. His fair skin accentuated the blueness of his freshly shaved face. He wore black dress pants and a baby blue dress shirt with his sleeves rolled up halfway, exposing his hairy arms. His shirt was buttoned down just low enough that the hair from his chest peeked out. His most significant appeal, though, was the light and kindness radiating from his smile, coupled with the calmness of his voice.

Entering his carpet shop, I plopped down on a heap of carpets and just stared at him with a smile that covered my face. He was talking, but I have no recollection of what he was saying. I was just fixated on him. It felt like a natural high, which made me giddy with excitement.

Interrupting him, I said with confidence, "Look, let me tell you how this is going to go. I will come back to Turkey to visit you. You will come to America to see me. But we're going to waste a lot of time going back and forth. Why don't we skip all that and just get married?"

It didn't matter that I knew nothing about him. He could have been married with children, or he could have been in a serious relationship. I didn't even know if he liked me. Maybe he preferred European women like many of the Turkish men.

He smiled and said, "Mmm ... okay, so you're crazy." Then he chuckled. "Amm, maybe we can have dinner first," he said in his sexy Turkish accent.

The voice inside my head—the one that's always talking—told me this was special. That sense of connection we felt with ease right off the bat made me unafraid to show my true colors. I knew I wouldn't be judged. There was an immediate sense of comfort we felt around each other, making it easier to relax into reciprocal states of vulnerability.

The electricity was like fireworks. Holding hands, we walked back to my hotel to freshen up. My spirit was dancing and whirling like the Dervishes of Konya.

We walked for about thirty minutes to Taksim Square, a shopping square with branches of cobblestone streets leading to shops and a multitude of bars and discos, all surrounded by an array of restaurants. He took me to a fish restaurant located on the first street. It had a balcony upstairs and indoor seating as well. He got us a table just next to the open kitchen where an older man was roasting eggplants and skewers of meat and a row of fish. He ordered us a grilled chupra dinner (Turkey's national fish, similar to sea bass), and a bottle of Raki.

Halfway through dinner, he murmured, "Mmm, so America?" He leaned back to relax and sipped on his drink. "What do you do in America?"

"I'm studying to be a doctor," I replied, gleaming with pride.

"Really? What kind of a doctor?" he asked.

"A psychologist," I said.

"Hmm, so you are analyzing me?" he asked jokingly.

"No, I don't work for free," I responded and laughed.

The older man cooking over an open-flame indoor oven brought out a roasted eggplant salad on the house. "Just for you," he said, looking like he was smitten with me.

I watched how gently my new love moved the food on his plate throughout dinner, picking it up and passing it to me first. He moved slowly and calmly, which matched the way he spoke.

Not wanting the night to end, I asked, "Do you want to go dancing after dinner?"

"Okay, let's go," he said in the calmest voice.

Grabbing my hand, he guided me over to club Jezebel. It was a crowded Saturday night, and the clubbing scene was alive. Many European older women with their younger Turkish boyfriends were out bar hopping. It was standing room only, but I didn't mind. We came to dance, not to sit down.

We jumped onto the dance floor to a reggae beat, then the Eminem hit song, "Cleaning Out My Closet." The young waiter found us a table for an extra tip. As soon as we sat down, he pulled up his chair next to me. Unexpectedly, he leaned in and kissed me.

My heart skipped a beat, and stars surrounded his head like a halo. Suddenly, we became the only two people in the room. Laughing, giddy from my natural high, and with the man who I knew was the last missing part of my puzzle. I felt alive and was having the time of my life.

As I packed for my return home the next day, scenes of our first meeting played like a movie in my head. But my logical and sensible head reassured me that there is no future with him. We lived on different continents and were from different cultures. I was ten years older and divorced with two children. All these doubts played in my mind. Yet, still, I couldn't get rid of this magical feeling. The feeling where everything suddenly became romantic and all I was able to see was love.

This is what falling in love feels like. I'm in love!

My heart exploded with a burst of energy—the excitement of the unknown and the possibilities that laid ahead.

Two months after returning to America, I arranged an extended vacation time with the children, celebrating my daughter's birthday in August. Then I left for the journey of my life.

Love, at first sight, is so real, but it's undoubtedly a complicated feeling. We were from different cultures and had different ways of practicing the same faith. My path in life was to practice non-judgment, and, in the process, I had learned acceptance. I spent a month with him in Sultan Ahmed, meeting his family, and making plans for our future. The Friday before I left, we decided to pray Jummah prayer at the Blue Mosque in Istanbul. After prayer, he took me to meet the Imam and asked if he would marry us according to Islamic rights. The Imam obliged, and we were married in the fifth century-old Blue Mosque. He made plans to come to the United States for Thanksgiving, my favorite holiday. It was only a couple of months away.

Returning to the States, life-changing news awaited me. Omar had gotten a spot to study martial arts at the Shaolin Temple in China. The two of us set off within the year for a one-month trip throughout China, including the Wudang mountains. Omar studied while I found my own Sifu to teach me Tai-Che.

Laila, now sixteen and emancipated, had decided to move back home with me. At school, she was part of the dual enrollment program and was awarded the chance to finish her last two years of high school at a community college. This would help her graduate high school early and receive an associate degree—the college was walking distance from my waterfront one-bedroom condo. My dream was to have my children return home to me one day, but I never really thought it was possible. The possibility of my son returning home in three years when he would be emancipated was real too. The search for my new home was on. This was not just a house, but a real home with my family. My new life, where I was in charge of my happiness. And it led to a three-bedroom, two and a half bath, split entry ranch in the suburbs of Boston.

And that was the beginning of my new life with the four people I love the most: myself, my two children, and my husband. I had again managed to create a beautiful life, and I was mindful of it every time my heart skipped a beat when I saw his car in the driveway.

Epilogue

"My mission in life is not merely to survive, but to thrive and to do so with some passion, some compassion, some humor, and some style." —*Maya Angelou*

Three years after my husband's arrived in the United States, I graduated with my doctoral degree in Pastoral Psychology.

My husband typically brought in the mail, dropping it on the kitchen island. But on this day, he walked in, and I was standing at the kitchen sink. He called out, "Jami, Jami, I think something came for you."

I had recently successfully defended my dissertation and was eager to find out the results. I ripped open the letter. From my readers, the dean, and the school's assistant dean: "Congratulations, Dr. Khan!"

It was the first time I was called Dr. Khan. It didn't even feel real.

In a larger envelope from my school was my diploma. I pulled it out, soaking in the official and surreal title. I had realized my life's dream of completing my doctorate. I let out a big sigh. I felt completed!

"What is it?" my husband curiously asked.

Turning the diploma around, I smiled and said, "Here, look."

He hugged me and said, "Congratulations, baby. You deserve it, but you have always been the doctor for my heart. I'm so proud of you."

I opted not to attend graduation; instead, I celebrated by doing something I love doing. I grabbed a friend and went back to Egypt for two weeks.

I've always seemed to have done things differently, and I learned to love and accept myself for my differences. I realized that I am different; I think differently and do things differently, which I considered a gift. In contrast, I've spoken to many women who've expressed, "I wish I could do this or that." I want to tell them they could, and at the same time, I realized that not many people are willing to do the necessary work it takes to be genuinely BE YOU!

As I reflect on my childhood and my life before, during, and after my first marriage, I am struck with immense gratitude. I've often wondered how I survived all the trauma. *Where did I get the strength to deal with all those challenges?*

My reflections turned into the realization that my faith and trust in God was what made me finally free enough to enjoy my life in the physical world.

The knowledge I've gained through my travels, education, and religious studies have made me a better person, one that most resembles the person I am meant to be. I want all the suffering people in the world to know that there's purpose in all things, your life included. There is purpose in your struggle. Have faith, and keep reaching for the stars because it's your life. Live it as you choose.

When I look at my children today, I see two well- educated and God-loving, contributing members of our society and great ambassadors to Islam. I'm reassured that I made the right decision to allow them the chance to learn and love Islam and accept other faiths.

My children came home to live with me when they turned sixteen and stayed until starting their own lives as independent adults. I love that the traveling bug has bitten them, and they travel the world every chance they get. They also continue to have a great relationship with their dad.

Twelve years after I met my second husband, I was faced with a dire diagnosis, one that nearly took my life, yet I survived. When I opened my eyes after thirteen hours of surgery and two days in a coma, the first people I saw were my two children, and behind them, my hayatum.

Aunty Kay was ninety-four when she passed away ten years after Grady; her mom died at age one hundred and four. Naani passed away at age ninety-two in 2005. And luckily, my mother is alive and doing well at age eighty-eight.

I published this book during the 2020 pandemic. This is a new level of collective trauma. The world is on lockdown, with much of the world closed off to U.S. citizens. Traveling, for now, is on hold. People have been experiencing severe anxiety and overwhelming fears of the unknown. The only way for me to make some sense of our world today is to look at it from the viewpoint of physics.

I believe that God created everything and everyone so perfectly, each with its own system to heal itself. Much like when we are sick, we throw up and then feel better even though our stomach went haywire for a bit, trying to readjust itself.

The world has been operating on a negative vibration with all the hate and destruction that had become the norm. The earth consists of energy like humans. Each human cell contains negative and positive energy (electron and proton) and stabilized with a neuron. We are all energy, and when we hate, we send out negative vibrations. The world became overloaded with these negative vibrations, and it has caused upheaval in an attempt to fix and stabilize itself. To heal itself, the universe needs positive vibrations.

This is yet another awesome reason to show love and compassion—the good and positive vibrations will help us and our earth to heal.

If we focus on the scope of the pandemic, we will be stricken with fear. It's like carrying the weight of the world on your shoulders. To deal with the immensity of this collective trauma, we all need to do our part. Start with the smallest circle, yourself, and take care of YOU. Then extend it to caring about your family, friends, community, and so forth.

The Beatles got it right with "All We Need Is Love"

Shaffick and Shairoon Mohammed

Contributors and Resources.

Editor—Val Cervarich
www.writinghelpkc.com

Photographer—Christine Demura
www.christine@familiphotography.com

Cover Design—www.100covers.com
Formatted and Printed by—www.FormattedBooks.com

Women & Shame: Reaching Out, Speaking Truths & Building Connection
Book by Brené Brown

Landmark Education
https://www.landmarkworldwide.com

Jamila Khan—www.PsychologyToday.com
jamilammk@yahoo.com
Whycantibehappy@gmail.com